MW01017438

EVEN TODAY

The Child is Father of the Man;
And I could wish my days to be
Bound each to each by natural piety.

William Wordsworth

Even Today

Theology and the Inner Child

DENNIS J. BILLY, C.SS.R.

ALBA·HOUSE   NEW·YORK

SOCIETY OF ST. PAUL, 2187 VICTORY BLVD., STATEN ISLAND, NEW YORK 10314

Library of Congress Cataloging-in-Publication Data

Billy, Dennis Joseph.
    Even today : theology and the inner child / Dennis J. Billy.
        p.   cm.
      ISBN 0-8189-0708-8
      BT702.B48   1995
      230 — dc20   94-45232
                                                      CIP

Produced and designed in the United States of America by the
Fathers and Brothers of the Society of St. Paul,
2187 Victory Boulevard, Staten Island, New York 10314,
as part of their communications apostolate.

ISBN: 0-8189-0708-8

© Copyright 1995 by the Society of St. Paul

Printing Information:

Current Printing - first digit	1	2	3	4	5	6	7	8	9	10

Year of Current Printing - first year shown

1995	1996	1997	1998	1999	2000

In memory of
my mother
Lillian Billy
(1927-1983)
for helping me find
the purest gold — even today.

Contents

Acknowledgments

Parts of this book have been published elsewhere: "Why a Redeemer? Why a Cross?" *Living Prayer* 26 (no. 2, 1993): 8-13 [reprinted here as Book VII: "What Happened to Him?"]; "Welcoming the Stranger: A Special Challenge for the 90's," *Pastoral Life* 41 (no. 10, 1992): 2-13 [reprinted here as Book VIII: "Welcoming the Stranger"]; "Befriended by Silence: Out of Awareness, into Rest," *Living Prayer* 24 (no. 5, 1991): 3-6 [reprinted here as Book IX: "Befriended by Silence"]; and "The Purest Gold," *Living Prayer* 20 (no. 2, 1987): 24-27 [reprinted here as the final Bookend]. Special thanks go to the editors and staff of *Living Prayer* and *Pastoral Life* for allowing me to incorporate these pieces into a larger work.

Introduction

I have talked to many people who feel out of touch with the child of their youth and long for a way of befriending their past. Troubled by the anxieties and misfortunes that overtook them as children, some have repressed their earliest experiences to the point of being unaware of them. Others have become conscious of them in varying degrees and are now searching for a remedy to cure them of their pain. Still others, like myself, have had a relatively happy childhood, but are more than a little embarrassed when it comes to revealing any part of it in their adult lives. The world we live in (so we tell ourselves) and especially the work we do has little room for the childish sentiments of youth. Preoccupied with what we call "matters of consequence," we make little time for the things that used to fascinate us in our earlier years. We turn to the Apostle Paul for reassurance: "When I was a child I used to talk like a child, think like a child, reason like a child. When I became a man I put childish ways aside" (1 Cor 13:11).[1] Easier said than done, even if it could and even if it should be done. Profound as they may be, even the words of the Apostle dwindle in significance when placed

---

[1] Unless otherwise stated, all quotations of Scripture come from *The New American Bible* (New York: Catholic Book Publishing Co., 1970).

beside those of the Gospel: "Unless you change and become like little children, you will not enter the kingdom of God" (Mt 18:4).

Even Today

My purpose in this book is to allow the child in me (and, I hope, in you, the reader) to surface in our thoughts about God, i.e., in the act of "faith seeking understanding" or "theology," as it is otherwise called. I am fully aware of the risks involved in such a task, not the least of which is that it will not be taken seriously and hence not read by those who probably need it the most — professional theologians. Risks, however, are made to be taken. For better or worse, I have made my decision and will live with the outcome, regardless of how others perceive me.

In struggling to allow my inner child to enter into the act of writing theology (he probably would have been much more at home smearing himself with finger paint), I have had to change many of my typically adult ways of doing things:

1. For one thing, I have had to return to the memories of my youth, many of which had long since receded from the reach of easy recall. Much of the effort involved here was simply waiting for the child in me to sift through my past experiences and to focus on the particular memory that he felt was most appropriate for the matter at hand. Since you, the reader, have only the final product before you, I ask you to be mindful of the many hours of thought and prayer that lie behind the words and memories which fill these pages.

2. In addition to memory, I have also had to rely a great deal on the powers of the imagination. I have tried to give the child in me free rein not only in the past, but also in the present. This has meant first allowing him to work with the various images that fill his mind and then translating them for him onto the printed page so that you, the reader, could benefit from his creations. It is

unfortunate that we adults have not learned to tap more deeply into the wonder-filled world of a child's imagination. If we had, we would not have created the unhealthy separation of the head from the heart which so dominates nearly everything we do. It is my sincere wish that some of what you read will help you to bridge this distance in your own life.

3. I have also found it necessary to complement the insights of the child in me with those of well-known poets and novelists. The authors of children's books also loom large in the pages that follow (probably because the child in me simply loves them so). Sooner or later, everyone's imagination runs dry and is in need of replenishing. The words of these authors convey what my inner child wished to say, but could not clearly articulate even with my help. Since I did not want my own limitations to keep the child in me from expressing himself as he saw fit, I had recourse to others who had already tapped into the world of their inner child and were able to bring its concerns to light in a creative and imaginative way. In doing so, I have tried to preserve the integrity of works cited and the sense (if not the setting) of their original contexts.

Memory, imagination, and literature are the three wells from which I have drawn water for the child in me to drink from and refresh himself. Although they are deep, and the work involved in bringing their cool, rejuvenating liquids to the surface was considerable, even more difficult was the task of first getting in touch with my inner child and then encouraging him to drink not once, but again and again. I overcame this obstacle by first writing and then committing to memory a poem about an old man remembering his childhood. "Even Today," which opens this assorted collection of short theological vignettes, was used day after day as a meditative point of departure for all else I have written. Its help to me was immeasurable. Whenever I felt lost or out of touch with the child in me, I was often able to reestablish contact by simply reciting this poem and entering into its spirit. It became for me a reliable way of awakening the child within me and calling forth his creative energies. I hope it will have a similar effect on you.

Bookends

Even the form this book has taken has been influenced by a childhood memory — at least in part. During the writing of it, the child in me began to focus more and more on a particular shelf on one of the walls of my boyhood room that was set aside for my favorite books. Through the years, the number and position of books on this shelf changed considerably. New ones were added; others were taken off and given to my younger brother and sister. When I look back on it, only two things remained constant: the bookends themselves that kept the books in place. There was nothing extraordinary about these unassuming knickknacks. They didn't even match: one consisted of three pieces of wood knocked together by my older brother back in his Cub Scout days; the other was an empty can of my father's Prince Albert's pipe tobacco that also served as a makeshift piggy bank. On the surface, they weren't much. They were mine, however, and they held my special little library in place. Without them, my books would have had nothing to keep them standing upright, and I would certainly have considered myself very much the poorer.

What you have before you is another assorted collection of "books" held in place by a dissimilar pair of "bookends." This time, both bookends are of my own making: one is the short poem, "Even Today" which, as I have explained earlier, seeks to capture the wonder of being a child through the reminiscing eyes of an old man; the other is a fairy-tale entitled, "The Purest Gold," which tells the story of a young boy who, through the enchanting touch of a rainbow, learns of the world's real riches when he is changed into a huge slab of granite rock. One is about the wonder of childhood;

the other, about the joys of contemplation and the wonder of growing old gracefully. Although they are dissimilar in both length and literary genre, they are very much alike in that each in its own way seeks to awaken the child within and allow him or her to assume a greater role in one's conscious awareness. I call them bookends because, together, they provide the childlike atmosphere one needs to assume before reading what falls between them. Without them, the work I am presenting would have little to hold its individual sections in place and you, the reader, would lose yet another chance to get in touch with your inner child.

On the Shelf

The chapters themselves are also of my own making. Between poem and fairy-tale come nine short reflections ("books," as the child in me prefers to call them) on a variety of subjects, ranging anywhere from the horrors of violence, fear, and failure to the more benign qualities of trust, self-giving, and hospitality. All of them have in some way been inspired by the child in me: whether it be a little boy's fascination with the world of make-believe, recalling a terrifying nightmare, feeling safely nestled in my father's arms, or listening to the quiet stillness beneath life's pregnant voices. Taken in their entirety, these "books" touch such topics as pretending, trusting, fearing, hurting, failing, giving, suffering, welcoming, and listening. Although this sequence of themes was the one deemed most appropriate by the child in me at this particular juncture in time, it is by no means the only one and not necessarily even the best. Like books on a shelf, they can be arranged and rearranged, read and reread, in the order one wishes. Think of them as your inner child's summer reading list. Such is the approach I have taken; I encourage you (and the child in you) to do the same.

I would ask, however, that you keep my bookends, "Even

Today" and "The Purest Gold," in mind as you browse or perhaps even systematically make your way through the books on my shelf. To the diligent and respectful reader, once a book is read, it should be put back on the shelf where it belongs. This normally does not happen without at some point having to handle the bookends themselves, even if it means only readjusting their positions or taking up some of the slack between the books. In the same way, I ask you, the reader, to be aware of what keeps the personal library that I am about to open up to you firmly in place and pleasing to the eyes. That is not to say that I expect you to reread each of them every time you chew on and digest one of the books it holds in place. I ask simply that you be conscious of their presence and respect the function they serve. Savor their taste, much as you would the slices of "Wonder Bread" in a peanut-butter and jelly sandwich or the deep chocolate wafers of an "Oreo" cookie. Eating and reading, after all, have very much in common. If you don't believe me, just ask Friar Tuck or any other monk worth his salt!

A Word on Subtitles

I have never seen a children's book with a subtitle (although I am sure I could find one if I looked hard enough). One has been supplied for this book, because the inner child for whom it is intended can be reached only through the eyes of the adult he or she has long since become. Adults, as we all know, have a strong propensity in most literary matters for such oddities as footnotes, parenthetical statements, and subtitles (I submit myself as a case in point). In this instance, the revealing phrase, "Theology and the Inner Child" has been selected for sound and appropriate reasons which nevertheless need some explaining.

To begin with, the word "theology" has many connotations and can be employed on many levels. I use it here not to give the impression that this work is of a scientific nature or to give it a degree of sophistication that it does not merit, but rather to underscore the fact that, in its broadest meaning as "faith seeking understanding" or "God-talk," the term can be applied to nearly everyone including little children. A person is a theologian to the extent that he or she has even a modicum of faith and seeks to clarify its meaning. My aim here is simply to free the word "theology" from the stranglehold of those who want to limit its use to purely scientific or otherwise academic endeavors. In doing so, I hope to highlight the sense in which all of us can be thought of as theologians (albeit in varying degrees).

Secondly, I realize that by using the phrase, "The Inner Child," I run the risk of having my book associated with current trends in psychology that use the same phrase in largely the same context and for similar ends. Just as this book is not a work of scientific theology, however, it is even less a work of popular psychology. My inspiration for the phrase "inner child" comes not from psychology or any of its popular subdisciplines, but from the Gospels themselves, particularly those which locate the Kingdom of God within (Lk 17:21) and assign entrance into it to those who become like little children (e.g., Mt 18:3; Mk 10:15; Lk 18:17). My usage of the phrase "inner child" is synonymous with "the child within" or "the child in me." I employ them interchangeably and do so strictly for stylistic reasons.

Finally, I would like to point out that the subtitle reads "Theology *and* [not *of*] the Inner Child." Perhaps I am stating the obvious, but I like the comfort that comes from being clear at the very outset. Nowhere in this book will you find anything at all resembling a systematic exposition of the theological dimensions of "inner childlikeness" (if I may be allowed to use a term of such "unchildlike" abstraction). All that is offered (and only those who seek it will find it) is an open invitation to allow the child in all of us to express him or herself in the act of "faith seeking understanding." It should not be surprising that the "God-talk" of the child within each of us may, from time to time, strike us as nothing but pure "baby talk." To our astonishment, however, there are other moments when it will move us with stirring insights into the meaning of our faith and the purpose of our existence. The words of Jesus himself highlight the childlike character of our deepest yearnings: "Let the children come to me . . . The kingdom of God belongs to such as these" (Mt 19:14).

Conclusion

If it is true that philosophy begins in "wonder," it would not be too far flung to suggest that theology, its spiritual kin and want-to-be queen, begins in "awe." I would go so far as to state that the child in me and the child in you are (or have the potential to be) masters of each of these related human sentiments. It is my firm belief, moreover, that our efforts in both disciplines will greatly improve if we nourish the inner child with the waters of life from which such experiences come.

Before I depart, I would like to draw your attention to the fact that I normally refer to my inner child in masculine terms. I do so not with the intention of being insensitive to the importance of inclusive language or of paying disrespect to individuals or groups, male or female. I do so simply because I think of the child in me in masculine terms and cannot easily do otherwise. In those places where I am not specifically referring to my own inner child and where I think the structure and/or style of the sentence does not suffer, I have tried to make adequate adjustments.

Other than that, for the moment, I invite you simply to grab a seat, kick off your shoes, and browse through the shelf of books I am about to place before you. "Enjoy!" as my father used to say when he would take us out after supper and buy us ice cream from the

Good Humor man. Read the poem; look at the fairy-tale. Examine what falls between them and decide for yourselves what you wish to open up to the eyes of the child within you. Better yet, let him or her decide what to do. "Everyone has to let go sometime." "Now is as good a time as ever." "What have you got to lose?" "The proof of the pudding is in the eating," as the old saying goes. I hope you find it to your liking.

Biblical Abbreviations

OLD TESTAMENT

Genesis	Gn	Nehemiah	Ne	Baruch	Ba
Exodus	Ex	Tobit	Tb	Ezekiel	Ezk
Leviticus	Lv	Judith	Jdt	Daniel	Dn
Numbers	Nb	Esther	Est	Hosea	Ho
Deuteronomy	Dt	1 Maccabees	1 M	Joel	Jl
Joshua	Jos	2 Maccabees	2 M	Amos	Am
Judges	Jg	Job	Jb	Obadiah	Ob
Ruth	Rt	Psalms	Ps	Jonah	Jon
1 Samuel	1 S	Proverbs	Pr	Micah	Mi
2 Samuel	2 S	Ecclesiastes	Ec	Nahum	Na
1 Kings	1 K	Song of Songs	Sg	Habakkuk	Hab
2 Kings	2 K	Wisdom	Ws	Zephaniah	Zp
1 Chronicles	1 Ch	Sirach	Si	Haggai	Hg
2 Chronicles	2 Ch	Isaiah	Is	Malachi	Ml
Ezra	Ezr	Jeremiah	Jr	Zechariah	Zc
		Lamentations	Lm		

NEW TESTAMENT

Matthew	Mt	Ephesians	Eph	Hebrews	Heb
Mark	Mk	Philippians	Ph	James	Jm
Luke	Lk	Colossians	Col	1 Peter	1 P
John	Jn	1 Thessalonians	1 Th	2 Peter	2 P
Acts	Ac	2 Thessalonians	2 Th	1 John	1 Jn
Romans	Rm	1 Timothy	1 Tm	2 John	2 Jn
1 Corinthians	1 Cor	2 Timothy	2 Tm	3 John	3 Jn
2 Corinthians	2 Cor	Titus	Tt	Jude	Jude
Galatians	Gal	Philemon	Phm	Revelation	Rv

BOOKEND

Even Today

When I was a child
I played by the sea,
And whiled away the day —
Merrily!
I built me a castle
And dug me a moat!
I made me a ship,
And I told it to float!
I picked me a pebble
That washed from a wave,
And polished a pearl
For my pocket to save!
I walked on a stretch
Of yellowish sand,
And found, there, the shore
Of a far away land!
I went with the wind
Wherever it blew!
I followed the birds of the air
As they flew!
I salted the sea!
I named every fish!
I swallowed the sky,

And I made me a wish!
I sat with the shells
When they sang on the shore!
I made peace with the crabs
When they grumbled for war!

But now that I'm old
And wrinkled and gray,
When I go to the sea,
I have little to say.
I sit on a chair,
And I take off my shoes,
And I rest in the sun,
Or I read today's news.
I may have a drink,
If the sun gets too hot.
But, go for a swim?
No, I'd rather not . . .
But I sometimes remember
Those days with a smile,
When a stone was a jewel,
and a step was a mile,
When a mound was a mountain,
and a puddle, the sea,
When the sky could be touched,
And when I could be me!
For a child subsists
On laughter and joy
To him, everything
Is a game or a toy!
His world is a world
Of wonder and play,
And that has a place in my heart
Even today!

EVEN TODAY

Book I

The Child in Me

He is at a construction site, so he has to wear a hard hat. You never know what can happen a hundred and fifty stories above street level. Far below, the sound of city traffic buzzes like a swarm of droning bees. The pedestrians stop and go as traffic lights change from red to green — and back again. This far up they look like ants of all different colors — red, yellow, black, white, tan. He squints his eyes as if to verify what he has just imagined. He can barely make them out. Then he opens them wide as he watches his workmen first moving large steel girders into position. Once secured, each is carefully bolted and welded into place. The day's work is almost done. His job is to oversee this project, which has been going on for years and is finally nearing completion. The tallest building in the world will look beautiful against the skyline of America's largest city. Manhattan will never look the same — and all because of him! Just then the cellular phone rings. He picks it up and answers it. The voice is that of a woman and sounds strong and clear, as though it were coming from an adjacent room: "Tommy! *Tommy*! Supper's almost ready! Put those blocks away and get washed up. Your father will be home any minute." After securing one final girder, Tommy calls his men together and commends them on a good day's work. He helps them stow their tools away and follows them into the lift that will take them down to the street. When they get there, he waves good-bye to each one saying, "Take care. I'll see you tomorrow." He then walks across the street to the City Diner and makes his way toward the rest room. "A man can get mighty dirty building skyscrapers," he tells the owner, "mighty dirty — and hungry too!" The owner does not seem to understand. Tommy smiles and then grins. With a playful look in his eyes, he inquires, "What are we having, Mommy?"

The Gift of Pretending

Children are known for their power of imagination. Place a child between the ages of five and ten alone in a yard full of toys (or without toys, for that matter) and watch what happens. In no time at all, he or she will be living high, seemingly lost, in an exciting, never-ending world of make-believe. That world will be as predictable and unpredictable, as safe and as dangerous, as daring and as matter of fact as the world we inhabit. What's more, they will be capable of sustaining their imaginations for long periods of time (seemingly hours on end!) without the slightest sign of fatigue. Children can pretend at almost anything. Fred and Wilma Flintstone are as likely subjects as Batman and Catwoman. Policemen and firemen are common objects of imitation, as are doctor and patient, Mommy and baby, Martian invaders (at least, when I was child) and, of course, the more generic "good guys and bad guys" motif. Adults are no match for the creativity of a child at play. The possibilities of pretending are seemingly endless.

When I was a child in the mid to late 1950's, my make-believe world revolved around the Walt Disney version of the legend of Davy Crockett, the famous frontiersman and four-term Congressman from Tennessee, who was killed at the battle of the Alamo in 1836 while fighting for Texan independence. My buckskins and coonskin cap were a familiar sight to the folks living in the whereabouts of Jefferson Avenue in Staten Island, New York. Old Betsy, my faithful Tennessee long rifle accompanied me wherever I went, as did two young foxes, Peter and Blackie, whom (as I was later told) only I was able to see. We had a grand old time. "Davy, Davy Crockett, king of the wild frontier!" I must have sung that song a thousand times and more! My friends and I hunted, fished, trapped, killed bear, blazed trails, and befriended Indians together — all within a stone's throw of my own front door. Once, when we decided to do some *real* exploring, we even got lost for a couple of hours. When we finally found our way back, I was embarrassed to learn that "Davy Crockett's" mother had all the neighbors out looking for him.

I could fill a book with similar tales of my childhood exploits as, I am sure, most of us could. There is no great secret why this is so: children just love to pretend. It's as natural to them as breathing and one of their main means of coping with the world around them. Without it, their world (and ours) would be a poorer place.

In the World But Not of It

Let us peer more deeply into the child's world of make-believe. There is little to lose and much to gain. We may be surprised at what a child can teach us once he or she utters the fascinating and near magical words, "Let's pretend." These words present a challenge to the hidden (perhaps neglected) child in all of us. Are we bold enough to let this child step forward without subjecting him or her to the scorn and ridicule of our more sophisticated adult standards? Can we pretend to be the children we once were and, in some sense, have always remained? Are we really pretending at all? Perhaps the child in us is our true identity. Perhaps we are merely pretending to be adults. Perhaps a little boy or little girl roams around inside of each of us. Perhaps, like Peter Pan in Never-Never-Land, we have refused to grow up because the child in us is afraid of entering fully into the world of adult relationships. A child follows a line of reasoning different from our own. Pretending and make-believe place him or her *in* the world, but not *of* it. It does so in a variety of ways.

1. *What makes pretending so much fun for a child is the challenge it presents of living in another world.* The inspiration for the makeup of that other world can come from almost anywhere — real life, movies, TV, comic books, a dream, or any combination of these. The possibilities are virtually endless, as limitless as the child's imagination. When pretending, a child creates a world of his or her own making. The people who inhabit it, the rules which govern it, the forces contending in it are all subject to the control of the child's will and improvisation. Living in this other world presents a cushioned context in which the child can act out some of the pent up fears and anxieties which he or she faces in real life.

2. *By entering this make-believe world, the child has the opportunity to project his or her personality onto a larger social sphere.* By playing doctor or dentist, he or she imagines what it would be like to be in the other person's shoes, giving the injection or drilling the tooth, rather than receiving them. By playing cook, he or she imagines what it must be like to actually prepare the evening meal instead of just eating it. The world of make-believe allows the child to experiment with the different social roles he or she has encountered so far in life. To do this properly, the child takes on the identity of the character he or she is trying to emulate. I really thought I *was* Davy Crockett when I was living in that now so long ago world of my own creation — loyal, noble, and brave. That is why I wanted to dress exactly the way Fess Parker did, the actor who made Crockett so very real for me.

3. *The challenge of living in another world, however, only goes so far.* Sooner or later it is time to go home. It may be getting dark

outside, or it may be time to eat, or do some chores, or concentrate on homework. As much as the child may want to go on with the serious business of pretending, something always manages to pull him or her back to reality. This reentry normally occasions a feeling of refreshment that enables the child to better respond to the sometimes overwhelming demands of growing up in the real world. The feeling of invigoration often spills over into other areas of life. The little boy who has successfully removed a tumor from his sister's Barbie Doll may be a little gentler with his sister the next time he teases her by trying to take the doll away. Little Tommy is probably not afraid of heights and, even if he is, will be sure to be very careful after supper when he climbs atop his tree house.

4. *True pretending presupposes an ability to distinguish between the real and the unreal.* Those who are best at the world of make-believe are precisely those who understand that it is a different world from the one they inhabit. When they return, they are aware of where they have been and of what they have left behind. That does not mean, however, that the characters they have imitated simply cease to exist. On the contrary, those whose personae they have assumed in their world of make-believe are really psychic projections of their own inner lives. The policeman and fireman, the bank robber, the street cleaner, the doctor, the housewife, the super-hero, the super-villain have all been internalized one way or another. The child brings them back to the real world as his or her constant (albeit unconscious) companions whom no one else can see.

5. *Finally, be it ever so slightly, a child leaves the world of make-believe with a different outlook on life.* The cast of characters that he or she has assumed during the early years of childhood (and with decreasing influence in the later years) have left their impression. They linger in the mind and the imagination, and influence the way a child interacts with the surrounding world. The child may respond by doing one of two things: he or she may (1) listen to the

voices and thus allow them to participate with all the other factors that go into making serious decisions in the real world, or (2) ignore them or (even worse) repress them because of a false sense of what being grown up really entails. The former is the way of integrating one's inner child into one's maturing life; the latter will lead only to an estrangement of the inner child from the developing self. It is up to each person to decide.

The Story of Don Quixote

One of the classic stories of someone living in a world of make-believe is that of Cervantes' picaresque novel of the early seventeenth century, *Don Quixote*. The tale follows the exploits of Alonso Quijano, a Spanish gentleman of moderate means and of late-middle age, who devoted so much of his time and effort to reading books of chivalry that eventually "his brain dried up" and he began thinking of himself as a young knight-errant charged with the impossible task of righting all the world's wrongs. Armed with crooked lance and ancient buckler, protected by his rusted armor and a makeshift cardboard helmet, Quijano mounts his old nag, "Rocinante" (in his eyes a valiant steed) and sets out one fair day as the determined fiery-eyed "Don Quixote de la Mancha," a courageous and valiant knight of the realm, whose sole purpose in life is to conquer whatever perpetrators of evil he encounters in the name of the beautiful Lady Dulcinea, the noble inspiration of his deepest dreams — actually a poor farm girl from a nearby town. The foil of Quixote's adventuresome but, otherwise, hilarious quest is his complaining and overweight squire, Sancho Panza, a perennial pessimist at heart, who, riding an ass at his master's side, remains throughout the novel Don Quixote's sole point of contact with the real world. From one incredible episode to the next, the unwitting knight charges ahead of himself into the path of injury and defeat.

Windmills are mistaken for lawless giants, a wayside tavern for an enchanted castle, hardworking, flour-faced millers for frightful monsters holding a captured knight as ransom in a heavily fortified fortress. Don Quixote's antique armor and meager military skills are rarely a match for the blows inflicted by his usually reluctant adversaries. With his wounds nursed time and time again by the fearful and easily panic-stricken Sancho, Don Quixote is able to sustain his chivalrous world-view in the face of seemingly insurmountable odds. Only at the end of the novel, when he is unable to defeat the treacherous Knight of the White Moon and thus break a magical spell that had been cast upon his sweet Dulcinea, do the boundaries of his ideal world collapse. At this point, an interesting character reversal takes place. Lying on his death bed, sad and heavy of heart, Don Quixote (now the tired and weary-eyed Alonso Quijano) admits the foolishness of knighthood and all tales of chivalry; filled with grief over the broken spirit of his dejected master, Sancho tries to flame the embers of his master's dying dream. He succeeds, in part. As anyone who has ever read Cervantes' novel can testify, the impossible dream of the poor knight-errant has, from one episode to the next, been slowly kindled and then set aflame in the heart of the reader. Even after his death, Don Quixote still lives.

At first sight, the story of this fallen knight-errant is about the consequences of pursuing a noble cause without the necessary means. Books of chivalry have filled Don Quixote's mind with tales of conquest and romance, but have failed miserably in instructing him how to defend himself properly with buckler and lance or to wield his sword with razor-like precision. Lacking in youth, strength, and military prowess, the real wonder of the tale is that the wandering knight actually lasts as long as he does. A lesser man, according to anyone's critical reckoning, would have given up long before.

A closer examination of the story, however, reveals an even

deeper dynamic at work. The author is really calling into question the traditional criteria that distinguish sanity from madness. All throughout the novel, Don Quixote is the one considered insane. From beginning to end, it is *his* rationality, *his* decisions, *his* verve and sense of purpose that are brought into question. But in the end, when Alonso Quijano, who previously had so thoroughly identified himself with the life and purpose of the noble Don, suddenly "comes to his senses" and repudiates all that Don Quixote ever believed in and stood for, Sancho (and, with him, the reader) is convinced that "some new kind of madness must have laid hold of him."[1] Don Quixote has made a deeper impression on his friends and followers than Alonso Quijano could ever have hoped for. Sancho even pleads with his dying lord: "Ah, master . . . don't die, your Grace, but take my advice and go on living for many years to come . . . Who knows but behind some bush we may come upon the lady Dulcinea, as disenchanted as you could wish."[2] What is it about the figure of Don Quixote which has so taken hold of one of the world's great pessimists? He has taken up the challenge of living in another world. He has encountered the dangers of this quest with uncommon bravery. He has had a deep moral effect on those who have journeyed with him. If he can be faulted for confusing the real with the imaginary, it may be that it was the only way of awakening the sleeping child in Sancho — and in all of us. If his "coming to his senses" and subsequent death meant his departure from the world of chivalry, it may be that it was only by death that he could have entered the hearts of his closest followers and, yes, inhabit the world of his readers. Which of these interpretations is correct? That is for the reader to decide.

---

[1] Cervantes, *Don Quixote*, trans. and ed. Samuel Putnam (Garden City, NY: International Collectors Library, 1951), 550.

[2] Ibid., 552.

The Imitation of Christ

Building skyscrapers, wearing a coonskin cap, and engaging lawless giants may seem a far cry from anything having to do with the message of Christ. Jesus claimed many things, but never to be living in a world of make-believe. The life he lived and the horrible death he suffered were real — not imagined. Much the same can be said of his closest followers — Peter, John, Mary Magdalen. Their eyes may have been turned toward heaven, but they were in no way pretending. Their feet, like those of their Master, were always planted firmly on the ground, even after that ground had radically shifted as a result of the Easter event.

What can be said then about the disciple's call to imitate Christ? "You have put aside your old self with its past deeds and put on a new man" (Col 3:9-10). "Your attitude must be that of Christ's" (Ph 2:5). "Be imitators of God as his dear children" (Eph 5:1). ". . . put on the Lord Jesus Christ and make no provisions for the desires of the flesh" (Rm 13:14). "Imitate me, as I imitate Christ" (1 Cor 11:1). Despite the reservations expressed above, certain parallels do arise between the disciple's imitation of Christ and the play of a child. "Imitation" and "pretending," after all, are two very closely related concepts; the two go hand in hand (or so it would seem) and in certain contexts can be used almost interchangeably. Perhaps a disciple takes on the attitude and mannerisms of Christ in a way similar to how a child adopts the attitudes and mannerisms of the character he or she is pretending to be. "Grace builds on nature," so the saying goes. Perhaps a child's pretending is nothing but a natural sign of what all of us are ultimately called to do on a higher plain in the grace and the Spirit of Christ. "Follow the way of love, even as Christ loved you" (Eph 5:2). "Unless you change and become like little children, you will not enter the kingdom of God" (Mt 18:3). Perhaps the child and the saint share more in common than has been previously thought.

Let us take a case in point. Jonathan Smith has just recently started going back to church and wants to take the call to discipleship seriously. He reads the Scriptures and learns that this involves adopting the attitude of Christ (Ph 2:5) in all things (Col 3:17). To do this, he tries to live his life with one simple question in mind: "What would Jesus do in this situation?" To respond appropriately in any given instance, Jonathan has to examine the circumstances at hand, identify the issues, recognize the parties in need, and imagine the role or stance Jesus would take in the matter. By trying to imitate Jesus (or, at least, his idea of who Jesus was and what he stood for), he slowly begins to act in ways contrary to some of his more surface inclinations. At work, he tries to be honest with his boss, when it would be much easier to lie. He refrains from spoiling the reputation of a co-worker by talking behind his back. He accepts responsibility for an embarrassing mistake, rather than taking it out on a subordinate. At home, he shows affection to his wife and makes time for his children. He listens to them, makes sure they know he loves them, and tries always to be there for them when they need him. All this is difficult, of course (especially at first), and he does not always hit the mark. He still gets irritated and is capable of great insensitivity to his family and friends. He has a terrible temper and sometimes has a little too much to drink. His imitation of Jesus, one might say, is sometimes good and, at other times, barely recognizable. Although he is tempted to do so at times, he never loses faith. His heart is in the right place and, much to his surprise, "putting on Christ" gradually gets easier and easier as time goes on — at least so he thinks. Life is never perfect, and he would be the first to admit it. He still stumbles every now and again (sometimes badly), and he deeply regrets when he momentarily reverts to his former habits. Why such remorse? Perhaps a better question is: Why not such remorse? Trying to act like Jesus has brought about by God's grace a gradual, barely recognizable change in Jonathan's character. It eventually gets to the point that he does-not understand himself apart from his imitation of Jesus. The actor is becoming one with his role. His character is slowly being fitted to the persona of Christ. The life he is living is not his own, but Christ living in him (Gal 2:20).

Granted that there still may be a very large discrepancy between Jonathan's *idea* of Jesus and who Jesus really is, one has to wonder if this process of conversion ever would have begun at all if, as a child, he had never once exercised his imagination and uttered the amazing, alluring, magical words, "Let's pretend." In his seeking to imitate Christ, Jonathan has done everything he ever did when he pretended as a child — and more. He has taken up the challenge of living in another world; he has projected his personality onto a higher plain; he has kept his feet firmly rooted on the ground; he has never lost touch with the distinction between the real and the imaginary; and he himself has been deeply changed by the experience. He has, in a manner of speaking, put on the armor of God, with the belt of truth, the breastplate of justice, the shield of faith, the helmet of salvation, and the sword of the spirit, the Word of God (Eph 6:13-17). Don Quixote never had it so good! The same can be said for all the other Jonathan Smith's of the world. "The kingdom of God belongs to such as these" (Mt 19:14).

Conclusion

Most of us are so busy with our sophisticated adult concerns that we have almost completely forgotten what it is like to pretend. We have lost touch with our powers of imagination and must now rely on others to do our imagining for us. We even cite Scripture to back us up (1 Cor 13:11) — albeit out of context. The result can be nothing but disturbing. We say we have outgrown the child's world of make-believe, but have put nothing in its place. How can we "put on Christ" if we have forgotten what it is like to build a skyscraper, wear a coonskin cap, joust with windmills — or the equivalent thereof? The challenge of discipleship has been blunted by our own lack of imagination. Because we have no dreams, we mistakenly believe that dreams can never come true. Worse yet, we scorn and mock those who dare to question our assumptions.

Jesus himself was once a small child and probably knew very well the meaning of the words, "Let's pretend." Even if we do not know what he imagined (i.e., who he pretended to be; what make-believe world captured his imagination, etc.), there can be little doubt that he acted and played like any other first-century Hebrew boy his age. He was like us in all things except sin (Heb 4:16), and few people, if any, would place the innocent imaginings of a child at play in the category of moral failure.

From what we know of him, it seems that Jesus' imagination affected his life of prayer and had a profound effect on the way he understood his relationship to God. Do we not see it shining through his parables of the kingdom, those fascinating oral vignettes that speak to us so powerfully of God's infinite love and mercy? Does it not also come through in the way he affectionately calls God "Abba, Father" (Rm 8:15), or in the amazement and thankfulness of the people he cured? Does not his message of the nearness of God's reign resonate with an immediacy that challenges our normal expectations of life? "All of that, plus more!" — as the saying goes. In three short years, Jesus lifted all of humanity to a higher plane. "I am not to be with you much longer" (Jn 13:33). "My kingdom does not belong to this world" (Jn 18:36). "Father, Lord of heaven and earth, to you I offer praise; for what you have hidden from the learned and the clever you have revealed to the merest children" (Mt 11:25). Most of us can ill afford to lose touch with the child we once were and, in many respects, still remain. To this day, Jesus beckons the child in each of us to open its arms to his love: "Let the children come to me. Do not hinder them" (Mt 19:14).

BOOK II

Sink or Swim

A boy of six holds on for dear life as his father takes him out into water over his head. He wants to learn how to swim, but he is afraid. Once last summer he had waded out alone into water just up to his waist and had gotten a bad scare when he momentarily lost his balance and choked on a mouthful of salt water. He didn't scream as an approaching wave fell over him and pushed him back toward the shore, but he was unnerved for a time at least until he could get back to his feet. He was too afraid to go out that far again. Even now he is apprehensive as he clings to his father's neck and ventures out to where his feet cannot touch bottom. The powerful waves make him feel small and vulnerable. He wonders if they are too big even for his father to handle. Low tide or no low tide, the waves seem mighty big to him, mighty big indeed.

They have made it past the breaking point of the waves. People are swimming by them, parallel to the shore. The boy's father is standing in water up to his neck. The boy holds on to his father even tighter as he stretches his toes downward and fails to touch bottom. "Trust me, son, there's nothing to be afraid of." The father slowly buoys his son up onto the surface of the water with one arm under his chest and the other under his waist. "Now, kick, son, kick." Feeling the support of his father's arms, the boy concentrates on what his father tells him. "Move them up and down, like a scissors and don't bend your knees!" At first it seems difficult, but he gets the hang of it after a while. "Okay, now move your arms one after the other over your head and then out toward the water." The boy does as his father tells him. "Don't stop kicking! Do them both at the same time." The boy focuses on his father's instructions: "Kick and swim! Kick and swim!" He eventually gets the gist of it, even though he feels as if he isn't going anywhere or, at best, getting there very slowly. After a while, he realizes that his father's arms are no longer supporting him. For a split second, he senses that he has been staying above water on his own power. Then fear overwhelms him, and he starts to sink. "Daddy! Daddy!" The boy's father catches him just as his head goes under water. He lifts him up out of the water and over his head. "You did it, son! You did it!" The boy is startled and coughing up a little water, but he hears what his father is telling him and he knows it's true. "Yeah, I did it! I was swimming, Daddy! Did you see me swim?"

The Wisdom of the Fox

The above scene comes out of my own childhood. I look back to it often not so much because it marks the beginning of my learning how to swim (a skill I am deeply grateful to have), but because it is the first time in my life that I understood in a concrete way what it meant for me to place my trust in another person. Learning how to trust is a basic skill which all of us need. It may be difficult for us to think of it as a skill, but that is precisely what it is: a way of acting that is acquired through practice over an extended period of time. If we fail to learn how to trust others, the quality of our lives is greatly diminished. Without trust, we live in isolation from one another. We look upon others with suspicion and are afraid to take the risk of asking them to be there for us when we need them. When we learn how to trust others, life is easier to live and a much happier affair. Trusting comes naturally to some (or, at least, so it seems); others have a harder time of it. This could be due to any number of things (e.g., family upbringing, a hostile social environment, a traumatic experience in one's youth or childhood).

The fox in Antoine de Saint Exupéry's classic children's tale, *The Little Prince*, provides some keen insights about how to go about building up trust in another. The little prince comes from a tiny little planet from far, far away. He encounters a wild yet learned fox, who teaches him an important lesson about friendship:

> "If you want a friend, tame me . . . ."
> "What must I do, to tame you?" asked the little prince.
> "You must be very patient," replied the fox.
> "First you will sit down at a little distance from me — like that — in the grass. I shall look at you out of the corner of my eye, and you will say nothing. Words are the source of misunderstandings. But you will sit a little closer to me, every day."[1]

The little prince tames the fox by coming back every day at the same hour to greet him. Little by little, they get to know and to trust each other. In time, the distance between them lessens as the bond between them grows.

The wisdom of the fox touches the heart of the matter. We develop a relationship of trust with another person by beginning with small seemingly insignificant gestures. These small, fortuitous signs help to create an atmosphere of familiarity which enables us to take down our guard and establish a relationship of mutual care and respect. When we reveal ourselves to another in this way, we form a relationship that is unique in all the world. In the present

---

[1] Antoine de Saint Exupéry, *The Little Prince*, trans. Katherine Woods (New York: Harcourt, Brace & World, 1971), 84.

situation, the wildness in the fox is tamed, while the little prince learns a very important secret: "What is essential is invisible to the eye." From this common realization, a lasting friendship is formed. For both the fox and the little prince, the world will never again be the same.

Crusoe and Friday

The same can be said for the main characters of *Robinson Crusoe*, Daniel Defoe's great adventure story of a shipwrecked sailor on a desert island. Crusoe and his man Friday are about as different as night and day. The former is an experienced seaman and God-fearing Christian who, finding himself stranded all alone on an island off the Atlantic coast of South America, must fend for himself with a limited amount of supplies and rations. The latter is a savage from one of the neighboring islands who is brought to the island by an enemy tribe and about to be killed and eaten when he is rescued by Crusoe. Himself a cannibal, who worships the god Benamuckee and who has values entirely different from those of "civilized man" (at least, as the phrase is understood in early 18th-century England[2]), Friday is seen by Crusoe as a gift of Divine Providence, a veritable answer to his prayers. At long last, God has blessed him with a servant and companion! The fascinating part of the tale to watch is how the two men, who start out deeply suspicious of one another, gradually grow attached to each other to form a close and lasting friendship. Circumstances are such that they are able to share each other's stories and learn from one another in order to make life easier on the island for both of them. Although Crusoe clearly holds a position of authority in the

---

[2] Although *Robinson Crusoe* was first published in 1719, Crusoe's fictional meeting with Friday takes place in 1683.

relationship (Friday starts out as his servant and slave and only gradually earns his freedom), the mutual feeling of respect and admiration that develops between them cannot be questioned. Crusoe comes to trust Friday so much that he teaches him about gunpowder and firearms, gives him a knife and hatchet to carry around with him on the island, and even offers to help him to return home. Friday's response to this last genuine offer of concern is more than a little surprising:

> He looked confused again at that word, and running to one of the hatchets which he used to wear, he takes it up hastily, comes and gives it me. "What must I do with this?" say I to him. "You take, kill Friday," says he. "What must I kill you for?" said I again. He returns very quick, "What you send Friday away for? Take, kill Friday, no send Friday away!" [3]

Friday feels so close to Crusoe that he would rather die than be separated from him, even if it means the chance to return to his native island and being reunited with his tribe. The two men have developed a strong bond of trust despite their differing customs, creeds, opinions, and other practical concerns. Even the color of their skin does not get in the way (an unusual happening for the early 18th century). What's more, Friday even chooses to follow Crusoe to Europe when, after many long years of loneliness and isolation, a passing pirate ship provides for their timely rescue.

Defoe's novel, often considered the first English novel, and which certainly numbers among the great myths of Western civilization, underscores not only our ability to survive seemingly insurmountable odds, but also the potential each of us has to transcend petty differences and to enter into a strong bond of

---

[3] Daniel Defoe, *Robinson Crusoe*, ed. Angus Ross (Harmondsworth, England: Penguin Books, 1965), 227.

mutual trust with another human being. From this perspective, the real adventure in the story is not Crusoe's remarkable feat of solitary endurance which lasts, by his own reckoning, some 28 years 2 months and 19 days, but the enduring friendship he is able to form with a person from a foreign land who speaks another tongue. The fact that Defoe's novel is partially based on the real life story of one Alexander Selkirk, a skilled Scottish sailor who beginning in 1714 was marooned on one of the Juan Fernandez islands, just off the Pacific coast of Central America, for a total of 4 years and 4 months, makes the depth of Defoe's message all the more relevant and engaging.

Learning to Trust

Given the above incidents from both fiction and real life about the meaning of human trust, a number of observations are in order.

1. *We tend not to trust each other because of our fear.* We are afraid of being let down; we worry about being hurt. We distrust others because we do not know them and are keenly aware of the pain that a single person is capable of inflicting on another. Fear breeds suspicion, anger, contempt, and a host of other negative attitudes. To justify it in our minds, we often accentuate our differences (e.g., race, religion, sex, nationality) and use them to form semi-sophisticated rationales for explaining the predominant lack of trust in our lives. Prejudice is an extreme form of distrust that is directed toward entire groups of people. Although we all are capable of dealing with others in this way, it comes much easier to those who have never learned how to trust someone.

2. *Before we can come to trust another person, we must first become aware of our fears and ask ourselves whether or not they are well-grounded.* Fear can be healthy or misconceived. In the former case,

it is a natural defense mechanism that warns us of immanent danger. Without it, we would not be able to avoid situations that would put our health and possibly even our lives at risk. In the latter, it is ill-conceived and not proportionate to the risk involved. This kind of fear turns us in on ourselves and paralyzes our ability to sustain authentic human relationships. Only by facing our fears — both the good and the bad — and making a realistic evaluation of them can we ever hope to deal with them effectively.

3. *Before we place our trust in another person, it is also important for us to determine whether he or she understands the boundaries of trust and how not to overstep them.* Making this judgment is not always easy, especially if we are emotionally involved in the decision. Not everyone is worthy of our trust. Dangerous people can do a great deal of damage to those who unwisely place their trust in them. Before we confide in another person, we must ascertain whether or not there is a reasonable possibility of our trust being received and maintained. Not to do so is to invite disappointment and almost certain future heartache.

4. *Trusting another person normally involves an element of risk.* Once we have determined whether a particular person is worthy of our trust, we then must decide if we want to let down our guard and extend to him or her our free offer of friendship. Such an offer usually begins with a small gesture of care, is followed by concrete acts of concern, and gradually opens the door to opportunities for deeper sharing. Those who, for whatever reason, are unwilling to take this all-important step, will never understand what it means to trust. Those who take the risk, however, make themselves vulnerable for a time and thus open themselves up to the possibility of being hurt. Most people who enjoy the privilege of holding another's trust will assert that the benefits usually far outweigh the risks.

5. *Authentic trust cannot exist if it is not in some way reciprocated.* One-sided friendship lacks the one thing that is basic to all healthy relationships, i.e., mutual concern. For this reason, it is important

for us to evaluate our relationships from time to time and to ask ourselves if those in whom we have placed our trust have taken the trouble to do the same with us. "Reciprocal," in this context, means not that the other person is acting toward us in exactly the same way as we are acting toward them, but that he or she has given to us a sense that our friendship is important and worth preserving. If we do not have this sense, then the quality of the trust we claim to share can be called into question.

6. *Finally, building up a solid relationship of trust with another person takes a considerable amount of time and effort.* There is no such thing as "instant trust" or a "ready-made" friendship. Those who spend their time establishing a genuine relationship of trust with another person will reap its benefits and joys for many years to come. This relationship of trust must not be ignored or in any way taken for granted. It must be worked at every day and started anew when problems or doubts arise about the degree of intimacy that is shared. To trust another and to receive another's trust in return is one of the greatest blessings a person can receive in life.

Walking on Water

The dynamics of trust come through very clearly in the Gospel story of Jesus walking on water (Mt 14:22-33). Jesus orders his disciples into a boat and tells them he will meet them on the other side of the lake. When the boat is several hundred yards off shore, strong head winds come and threaten to capsize it. In the middle of the night, Jesus approaches them on the water. The disciples believe they are seeing a ghost and are filled with fear. Jesus himself tries to calm them down by telling them not to fear: "Get hold of yourselves! It is I." Peter alone musters enough strength to trust the Master's words: "Lord, if it is really you, tell me to come to you across the water." Jesus bids him to come. Peter gets out of the boat and begins walking on the water toward Jesus. When he realizes how strong the wind is, however, he becomes frightened and starts to sink, crying out, "Lord, save me!" Jesus stretches out his hand and catches him saying, "How little faith you have! Why did you falter?" When they get back into the boat, the wind dies down.

Jesus' disciples already trust him a great deal. They have left everything to follow him: home, family, possessions. They enjoy being in his company and follow him wherever he goes. Up until this point, however, they have not yet been put to the test. The violence of the storm, Jesus approaching them on the water, their heightened fear change things considerably. They have trusted Jesus in the past, but never in a situation like this. Most of them are unable to get beyond their fear. Peter alone is able to step out in faith, but even he seems to falter. As he gets out of the boat and slowly makes his way toward his Master, fear overwhelms him and he starts to sink. When he cries out for help, Jesus grabs hold of him and helps him back into the boat. When the incident is over, one gets the distinct impression that the trust shared by Jesus and his disciples in the boat is much deeper than before. Amazed by what they have just experienced, they reverence him saying, "Beyond doubt you are the Son of God."

Trusting another person tells us a lot about ourselves. Peter's courageous (albeit imperfect) act of faith reveals what is really important to him in life. By stepping out of the boat during the storm, he leaves behind what little concrete security he has left in the world. As he ventures out on the water, all he has to rely upon are the words of Jesus himself. Therein lies the balance between life and death. It is even possible that others in the boat, convinced that they are seeing a ghost, try to hold him back or, at the least, persuade him to doubt the reality of what he sees and hears. All to no avail. Peter risks his life to see if Jesus' words are stronger than the force of strong head winds and the power of the raging storm. His decisive act of faith gives his Master the opportunity to show everyone in the boat the true power of his love. By catching him and helping him back into the boat, Jesus tells Peter and the rest of his disciples that he will be there for them when they need him: to help them, to comfort them, to still their every storm. It is there, in the boat, with Jesus at his side and the rest of the disciples gathered around him, that Peter understands (perhaps for the first time in his life) what it means to be a man of faith.

Like Peter, we all have the capacity to sink beneath our fears or to rise above them. The choice is ours to make. If we allow our fears to overwhelm us, then we will never fathom the true depth of our human potential. We will always be reacting to other people on the basis of our mistrust and suspicion of them. If we rise above our fears, however, we will give other people the opportunity to be a part of our lives and vice versa. Life is too precious and far too short to deprive ourselves of the warmth of authentic human trust. Better to take the risk of living and being hurt than remaining isolated from others in the security of our private fears. Such is the wisdom of the fox. Such is the lesson learned by Crusoe and Friday. Such is the invitation extended to each one of us by Jesus when he walked on the water.

Conclusion

An authentic trusting relationship will last a lifetime. Occasionally, we may find ourselves in situations where we begin to doubt the strength of what we have always thought of as our most stable and lasting friendships. When this occurs, we must be willing to step out in faith and cry out for help when we find ourselves sinking. Trusting another person is never a static affair. It encompasses not only the ordinary ups and downs of life, but also those difficult situations that test the strength of our resolve and make us question our ability to go on trusting. These latter instances provide us with a unique opportunity to discover the real depth of our love. They invite us to push back the boundaries of hope and give us a deeper awareness of ourselves and the people we trust.

Trusting is a basic ingredient of all healthy human relationships. It enters into just about everything we do and is an important measure of the quality of life we lead. Knowing who to trust and when to trust and how to trust is just as vital to our lives as knowing when to speak and when not to speak — perhaps even more. It is hard to think of a situation in life where trusting another person does not somehow come into play. Perhaps this is so because we are social creatures by nature and have survived down to the present day precisely because we have learned what it means to rely on one another especially in times of danger. One could go so far as to say that the level of trust within a particular group — be it the family, the local community, the city, or the country — gives a clear indication of its true moral caliber. A society is human to the extent that it is trusting. Take away its ability to engender an atmosphere of genuine trust and the whole moral fabric of society becomes undone.

I am very happy that my father took me out that day into water over my head to teach me how to swim. I never would have gone, if I did not already place a great deal of trust in him. Through the experience of it all, I came to trust him even more. Braving the waves with my arms around his neck, fearing the power of the surf and undertow, feeling the support of his arms beneath me, these and other memories flood my mind from time to time and are accompanied by a deep sense of gratitude. On that day long, long ago, my father did more than merely teach me the rudiments of swimming. He showed me, for the first time in my life that I can clearly recall, the meaning of the word "trust," a lesson which, since that day, I have patiently learned many times over (albeit in different ways) and will not soon forget.

Book III

The Fears That Haunt Us

A little girl makes her way down the deserted, dimly-lit street. Street lamps cast a dull hue of yellow across her path. The moving shadows play on her mind, changing direction and shape with every step. The darkness heightens her senses. Every sound is amplified and perceived as a threat. She feels lonely and afraid. Won't anyone accompany her home? A noise suddenly startles her from behind. A footstep. Someone is following her. She picks up her pace. At the corner, she takes a quick look behind and makes out a solitary figure stalking her in the moonlight. She turns the corner and starts to run. Home is just a few blocks away. No sooner does that thought cross her mind when another figure steps out from the shadows in front of her. She stops dead in her tracks, then dashes to her right only to encounter yet another threatening shape. Suddenly she is surrounded. A host of malevolent shades encircles her and slowly tightens its noose around her neck. She closes her eyes and screams. The shadows consume her and, for a moment, she does not know where she is. Then, all is calm. She opens her eyes and finds herself dripping wet from the hot summer night, her moistened bed sheets wrapped around her neck. She closes her eyes again, this time not from fright but relief.

Recurring Nightmares

Each of us probably knows what it is like to have a nightmare. These unwelcome nocturnal intruders can come at any time in our lives, from when we are still being rocked in the cradle to our last living moments. They can be about almost anything: pursuit and capture, not being able to find one's way, a sense of loss or betrayal, the fear of death — to name just a few. Every nightmare is different. Each has a unique story (if its normally loose association of images and ideas can be referred to as such) and affects the dreamer in a personal way. Nor is there any easy way of determining what the connection may be (if there is any) between the nightmare and the dreamer's conscious life. Perhaps it is the way the unconscious processes certain repressed emotions that the dreamer has been unwilling (or unable) to face. Perhaps it has something to do with his or her psychic life. Perhaps it is a veiled call for help. The meaning of the dream can be known only to the dreamer; others can be of only secondary help. In the face of this deeply personal road to discovery, one thing is certain: nightmares are disturbing experiences. The relief of waking up from one is rarely proportional to the fright it instills, especially when the nightmare is recurring.

During the course of my grammar school years, I had a nightmare that came back to me a number of times. I am walking home from school and suddenly get a strange feeling that someone is following me. I turn around and see no one. A few steps further, I turn around again and still see no one. The feeling does not go away, and so I continue acting this way until, finally, I notice an Indian's feather sticking out from behind a telephone pole. I start getting scared, so I begin walking at a quicker pace. After a while, I turn my head again and notice several Iroquois scouts stalking me at a distance. I then start running as fast as I can. At that point, all hell breaks loose. An entire war party of forty or fifty braves comes out from hiding and starts shooting arrows and throwing knives and tomahawks at me. Their cries send a blood curdling chill down my spine. Projectiles are falling all around me as I run for dear life. They want to kill me, and I am not about to stop and ask them why! Somehow or other, I manage to arrive home in one piece. The big question is whether they will be out there waiting for me the next morning when I leave for school.

The nightmare never continues long enough for me to find out. It does, however, have a number of interesting variations. In one dream, the Indians pursue me home and then disperse. In another, I remember peeking out of my bedroom window and noticing a number of their headdresses moving behind a row of hedges that lined the front yard of the house across the street. In yet another, they actually try to get into my house by breaking down the doors and crawling through the windows. On that occasion, the only way I was able to keep them out was by waking up, something I had no control over at the time. I became so scared that it was impossible for me to continue sleeping. It was fear that had saved my life.

It took me a long time to understand the meaning of these disturbing nightmares. At first, there was a persistent temptation simply to shrug them off as occurrences totally unrelated to my waking life. Like Ebenezer Scrooge in Charles Dickens' *A Christmas Carol*, I took them for poorly digested bits of meat or cheese. They frightened me to no end, but there was no way I was going to take them seriously. Unfortunately, like Scrooge's own frightful apparitions they would not leave me in peace. Worse still, they followed me into my daylight activity and stalked me wherever I went on the periphery of my consciousness. Only years later did I realize that this recurring nightmare was all about my fears of school and the uneasy, disquieting feeling I had about my formal education.

The Iroquois in my dream correspond (much to my present embarrassment) to the typical Hollywood stereotype. Wild and ruthless savages, they aroused fear wherever they went and symbolized for me my inability to master the subjects I was studying at school. Math, Science, English, History and a horde of other hostile subjects followed me home each day from school and would not give me a moment's peace. They represented all that up to that point in my life I had experienced as wild, unruly, and generally beyond my control. Even at home, the fear they had awakened did not subside. Their chilling war cries haunted me even in my dreams. I began to see that fear of being overwhelmed by my schoolwork had been a primary motivating factor throughout most of my early education. I did not understand why I perceived my studies as inherently hostile. There probably were a number of reasons: lack of confidence, fear of failure, competition with my peers, subtle pressures from my parents, to name a few. All I can say is that deep down inside I felt as though I was under constant siege by hostile Indians, and I had not the slightest clue of how to go about making peace with them. With little or no hope of rescue in sight (the U.S. cavalry never appeared on the horizon), no wonder these dreams came back again and again to haunt me. When they finally did cease near the middle of the eighth grade, it was because I had lived with the fears for so long (shedding more than a few public and private tears in the process) that I had, by that time, become comfortably numbed to their cumulative effect. Besides, with my grammar school experience finally nearing an end, I began to realize that the subjects I had been afraid of for so long were not as ominous as my imagination had made them out to be. Somehow, I had always managed to survive. I never once lost my scalp.

Tapping the Unconscious

There is nothing unusual about the nightmare I have just shared. Despite its special meaning for me, it probably bears marked resemblances to some of your own dreams and what you have gone through to understand them.

1. *It belabors the obvious to say that all nightmares deal in fear.* A bad dream is not a bad dream if it does not in some way instill in us a sense of terror, dread, and foreboding. Nightmares sail through our sleep on the shifting winds of fear. They provide our unconscious with the opportunity to concretize through images, sounds, tastes, emotions, even touch, those fears that lie beneath the surface of our awareness. Very often they deal with those fears that we have refused to face and own up to. Because we have buried them alive in the soil of our unconscious, they rise up to haunt us during our sleep, the time when our conscious guard is down and the shadow side of our personality is more likely to reveal itself.

2. *Sustained by fear, nightmares ultimately center on that which terrifies us the most, i.e., the inevitability of death.* Anna Ivanovna of Boris Pasternak's *Doctor Zhivago* says it best:

> "Death is hanging over me. . . . It may come at any moment. . . . When you go to have a tooth out you're frightened, it'll hurt, you prepare yourself. . . . But this isn't a tooth, it's everything, the whole of you, your whole life . . . being pulled out. . . . And what is it? Nobody knows. . . . And I am sick at heart and terrified."[1]

We are terrified by death because it represents the unknown. Nightmares take advantage of this vulnerable spot in our nature. We never know when one will strike. We rarely can anticipate its outcome. We are afraid we (or someone close to us) is going to die. Who? What? Where? When? Why? Nightmares always keep us guessing.

---

[1] Boris Pasternak, *Doctor Zhivago*, trans. Max Hayward and Manya Harari (New York: Pantheon Books, Inc., 1958), 59.

3. *Nightmares do more than simply frighten us.* Because they deal with repressed fears and emotions, they are often designed to convey a message to our conscious selves. Whether or not we uncover that meaning will depend, to a large extent, on the seriousness with which we treat them. Every nightmare provides an opportunity for us to learn more about ourselves. It is easy to brush it aside (like our friend, Scrooge) with circumstantial complaints that have no real bearing on the cause of why we have become so frightened by what we have dreamed. The more difficult thing to do is to stay with the dream, rather than attempt to put it out of our minds; to ponder it, rather than place it in contempt. Every nightmare sends a unique signal from our psyches to our conscious selves. To discover its meaning, we have first to believe that meaning is there to be found through careful reflection.

4. *The meaning of a nightmare usually does not reveal itself all at once.* At first, the dreamer is usually too overcome with fright to be concerned with whatever significance the dream may have for his or her life. When this initial fear subsides, the dreamer must then decide whether the dream has more than mere surface meaning for his or her life. Sometimes he or she may have nothing more than a strong impression or a hunch to go on. Not all dreams can (or should) be treated with the same amount of attention. Some are more important to the life of the dreamer than others. At this point, the arduous task of reflection begins. Details are remembered and reflected upon. Images from the dream merge with memories from the past. A pattern gradually emerges between the dream and the dreamer's conscious life. This may involve similarities between the dream and actual circumstances from the dreamer's daily life or, as is more likely the case, attitudes, fears, and disgruntled hopes long since buried and forgotten. Nightmares provide the occasion for the dreamer to come to terms with his or her repressed past. If the opportunity is seized, the dreamer will be blessed with a deeper insight into his or her life.

5. *Finally, the nightmare often carries with it an invitation to change.* Once committed to the process of reflection, the dreamer must carry over his or her newfound insight into the circumstances of daily life. He or she now must take up the challenge of facing the fear that has risen to the surface of consciousness. This once submerged anxiety now bids the dreamer to address those situations which seek to perpetuate its continued repression. Even though a nightmare has occasioned the emergence of this fear from the unconscious to a person's conscious state, there is no guarantee it will be dealt with effectively. Deliberate action must be taken to insure that the message of the dream is in some way carried out. This final step from insight to action is, by far, the most difficult in the entire process. Those who fail to take it are worse off than they were when they first began. Having encountered their fears and having come to understand them (perhaps for the first time in their lives), they still prefer to wander down the path of self-deception. They refuse to see that fears must not only be named, but also faced.

The Legend of Sleepy Hollow

Ichabod Crane, the lanky schoolmaster of Washington Irving's classic tale, "The Legend of Sleepy Hollow," is a typical example of a man unable to face his innermost fears. Endowed with a vivid imagination and a superstitious mind, Crane cultivated an insatiable appetite for the extraordinary. When school was out and he had time to spend on his own intellectual pursuits, he would often lie down in a field of clover near his one-room schoolhouse and immerse himself in the finer details of Cotton Mather's *History of New England Witchcraft.* As Irving describes him, "No tale was too gross or monstrous for his capacious swallow."[2] That is not to say

---

[2] Washington Irving, "The Legend of Sleepy Hollow," in *The Complete Tales,* ed. Charles Neider (Garden City, NY: International Collectors Library, 1975), 36.

that Ichabod was not frightened by the haunting stories he filled his head with. On the contrary, on his way home after dusk along the dark, winding country road that led from the schoolhouse to his lodgings in a farm house on the outskirts of town, he found more than enough fearful tinder for his overactive imagination to kindle and set aflame. Every sound of nature — the hoot of an owl, the sound of a whippoorwill, the rustling of trees — suddenly became a sullen harbinger of death and destruction. Every turn along the dark, solitary path home concealed unknown dangers, ghosts, goblins, witches, and demons. The possibilities were endless, and that made poor Ichabod all the more frightened.

Of all his fears, Ichabod was especially afraid of meeting up one night with the infamous Headless Horseman of Sleepy Hollow, the ghost of a Hessian soldier from the American Revolution who, according to local legend, had lost his head to a passing cannon ball and now haunted the deserted roads of the region atop his black military stallion. On one occasion, the encounter actually took place (or so our superstitious schoolmaster seems to have convinced himself). Coming home late one evening from a dance where he had been turned down by the daughter of a wealthy Dutch farmer in favor of a daring young farm lad named Brom Bones, Ichabod and his horse Gunpowder, a powder-gray nag he had borrowed for the evening, were pursued for miles on end by a tall dark figure on a galloping steed who held in his hands a large round object that could easily be mistaken for a head. When they reached the wooden bridge near the neighborhood church, a place where Ichabod thought he might find refuge, the Phantom Horseman finally pulled within range of his prey and hurled his severed head with one heavy swoop, hitting the terrified schoolmaster on the noggin. The next morning, not a trace of Ichabod was to be found — only his hat, and a shattered pumpkin close beside it.

No one quite knows for sure what happened to the unfortunate schoolmaster. Some say he was carried off by the Galloping

Hessian. Others insist that he had survived the incident, but had left the neighborhood partly out fear of the Horseman and partly because he was mortified at being dismissed by the girl he loved. Still others believe that he was spirited away by some supernatural means. The author leaves the distinct impression that Brom Bones, Ichabod's main rival for the hand of the farmer's daughter, staged the entire incident and that it was he who targeted the pumpkin for Ichabod's head. However Ichabod interpreted the incident, one thing is clear: for all his learning in matters pertaining to witchcraft and superstition, he had never learned how to face his fears. His decision to flee both home and livelihood confirms that he was still haunted by whatever he experienced on that fateful autumn night and would continue to be thus tormented wherever he went. Ichabod left town that night a lonely wayfarer on the shadowy road of self-deception; the Headless Horseman was still pursuing him.

The Last Temptation of Christ

At times, each of us walks in the footsteps of Sleepy Hollow's ignoble schoolmaster, perhaps being only vaguely aware that we really should be following those of another. The way of Jesus, unlike that of Ichabod, challenges us to face our deepest fears and anxieties. We know this because Jesus himself is said to have struggled with the inner voices of self-deception.

The fears that haunt us tell us much about ourselves; the way we react to them, even more. Nikos Kazantzakis' novel, *The Last Temptation of Christ*, develops this simple theme in a noble (albeit controversial) fashion. As the story goes, Jesus' greatest temptation comes not in the desert when the devil tries to lure him with promises of pleasure, power and possessions (Mt 4:111), but when he was dying on the cross and utters the heart rending words, "Eloi, Eloi, lama sabacthani?" ("My God, my God, why have you forsaken

me?" Mk 15:34). After the first two words, which invoke the name
of the Lord Sabaoth, Jesus faints for a short time — a matter of
seconds — and dreams of coming down from the cross, having his
wounds nursed by Martha and Mary, marrying them, and raising a
family which he supports by doing what he knows best, i.e., building
wooden chests and furniture. The dream is so real that Jesus actually
believes it is taking place. His wounds heal; his wives and children
love him; his business flourishes. He is living a life that any man
would envy. All he wants to do is lead an ordinary life and not be
bothered by the memories of his previous life as a prophet and
would-be Messiah. He does a fairly good job of forgetting, until,
years later, when he is old and gray, his disciples return to remind
him. Gray, balding, and lined with age, they proceed one by one to
taunt him for abandoning them. Judas Iscariot epitomizes their
complaints:

> "What business do you have here? Why weren't you
> crucified? Coward! Deserter! Traitor! Was that all you
> accomplished? Have you no shame? I lift my fist and ask
> you: Why, why weren't you crucified?"[3]

Jesus agrees. After listening to the charges of those who followed
him so many years ago, he feels ashamed of himself:

> "I am a traitor, a deserter, a coward. . . . Now I realize it: I'm
> lost! Yes, yes, I should have been crucified, but I lost
> courage and fled. Forgive me brothers, I cheated you. Oh,
> if I could only relive my life from the beginning!"[4]

---

[3] Nikos Kazantzakis, *The Last Temptation of Christ*, trans. Peter A. Bien (New York: Simon and Schuster, 1960), 492.

[4] Ibid., 494.

The accusations of his disciples do not stop: "One by one they shouted, 'Coward! Deserter! Traitor!' — and then vanished."[5] In the next instance, Jesus is alone. He feels terrible pains in his hands and feet. He utters the remaining words, "Lama sabacthani." His head quivers. Suddenly he awakens from his dream and remembers where he is, who he is and why he feels pain: "A wild, indomitable joy took hold of him. No, he was not a coward, a deserter, a traitor. He was nailed to the cross. He had stood his ground honorably to the very end; he had kept his word."[6]

The point of the novel (one often missed by those who protest some of its more sensational aspects) is that Jesus has faced the powers of self-deception and withstood them. The temptation to come down from the cross haunts him to his final breath, but ultimately fails to weaken his Messianic resolve. Spirit conquers flesh. Jesus confronts his deepest fear and overcomes it. By remaining on the cross, he fulfills his destiny. He awakens from his final nightmare with a deeper insight into the meaning of his suffering and death: "He uttered a triumphant cry: IT IS ACCOMPLISHED! And it was as though he had said: Everything has begun."[7]

Conclusion

In the prologue to *The Last Temptation*, Kazantzakis claims to have written not a biography, but "the confession of every man who struggles."[8] He uses a highly imaginative portrayal of Jesus to convey to his readers a very profound truth of human existence: if we do not confront our fears, we will forever be running away from

---

[5] Ibid., 495.

[6] Ibid., 496.

[7] Ibid.

[8] Ibid., 4.

them along the path of self-deception. Scripture puts it another way: "Love has no room for fear; rather, perfect love casts out all fear. And since fear has to do with punishment, love is not yet perfected in one who is afraid" (1 Jn 4:18).

Such fears differ from individual to individual and have both objective and subjective aspects to them. Whatever they may be — walking home in the dark, being overwhelmed by school, being intimidated by a rival, letting down those you love — these fears will continue to haunt us in our dreams and stalk us on the periphery of our consciousness until we finally choose to confront them and make peace with them. The concrete manifestation of these fears can be almost anything: shadows on a dimly lit street, Iroquois braves on the war path, a galloping Hessian soldier, cantankerous old apostles — you name it. In the long run, it is not so much what concrete shape these fears take, but the message they seek to convey to us. Of even more importance is the way we respond to them and the change that occurs in us as a result.

By most counts, we will continue to be frightened by the fears that haunt us. Nightmares have been around a long time and give no indication of going away soon. The question is not whether we will have them, and certainly not whether we will be frightened by them, but how will we handle them. Let the dreamer beware! Every nightmare carries with it both an invitation to change and an accompanying risk of yet another opportunity lost. The choice is ours to make: The way of self-knowledge? Or the way of self-deception? For Kazantzakis, it was clear what road Jesus had taken: "Temptation fought until the very last moment to lead him astray, and Temptation was defeated. Christ died on the Cross, and at that instant death was vanquished forever."[9] And for all this, Jesus and all who followed in his path were deeply blessed by God. Our world, and the fears which haunt it, would never be the same.

---

[9] Ibid.

Book iv

The Beast Within

We stalked our tiny prey in the still morning air as it fluttered from branch to branch in a nearby grove of sapling oaks. Our leader cradled the oversized rifle in his small boyish arms. Pellets, at close range, could be just as deadly as bullets at least for what we were hunting. The nine of us watched in silence as Jimmy drew within range of his target, raised the rifle to eye level, adjusted his sights, took careful aim, and gently squeezed the trigger. A short thunderous burst sent a tiny bead of lead hurling through the air. The pellet hit its victim just below the beak. The sparrow closed its eyes and bent its head instinctively in a belated attempt to ward off its deadly wound. It faltered for a second or two, as if the wind had momentarily caught it off balance. It then lost its grip, and fell to the ground. It was dead before impact. "I got it! I got it!" Jimmy screamed over and over, as he raised his rifle over his head and stamped his feet around his prize in an unrehearsed victory dance. His bloodcurdling cry echoed through the woods and drew all of us into a near savage state of frenzy. The blood rushed to our faces as we surrounded our vanquished prey and howled like a pack of hungry wolves: "Ahhhooooooooo! Ahhhooooooooo! Ahhhooooooooo!" The next instant saw us passing the rifle from one to the other, as each fearless hunter got his

own chance to dance around the bloodied carcass and fill it full of
lead.

Complete Annihilation

The above scene really happened — to me. I remember quite
vividly the time when my friend Jimmy got a BB gun for his 10th
birthday and how a group of us went up to the woods of Todt Hill
early one Saturday morning to try it out. We started looking for
squirrels and chipmunks, but eventually settled for anything that
moved. The sparrow, the unfortunate recipient of our youthful
enthusiasm, just happened to be in the wrong place at the wrong
time. We shot it dead not once, but several times — and for no good
reason. Some cruel and savage instinct had swept over and taken
control of us. One shot was not enough. Each of us wanted to pull
the trigger himself and watch it die again and again in his mind.
Lost in the thrill of the hunt, we needed at least thirty pellets to do
the job to our satisfaction.

Only afterwards, did it occur to me that, in different circumstances, any one of us could be taken unawares like that unsuspect-
ing sparrow. I understood something of what it meant to bear the
brunt of another man's fury. Still worse, there was something
cowardly, almost cold-blooded, about what we had done. The more
I thought about it, the more ashamed I was of the way we had
relished in the kill. We wanted not only the death of our prey, but
its complete annihilation. We wanted to spill its guts and watch its
blood mingle with the dust of the earth. We wanted to take what
we could not give and give what ultimately would take us all. The
line between life and death had become so thinly drawn for us,
almost indistinguishable. We were walking a tightrope and the gun
in our hands was what we were using to maintain our balance — or

so it had seemed. That day I sensed a strong primitive instinct lurking just beneath the surface of my skin. It would take very little, I thought, for this ignoble savage to direct its destructive wrath towards another human being — very little indeed.

Cry of the Hunters

I am reminded of William Golding's tragic tale of lost childhood innocence, *The Lord of the Flies*. A group of boys are stranded on an island somewhere in the South Pacific. Lacking adult supervision, they try their best to follow the moral tenets they had been bred to follow ever since they could remember. They begin with some degree of success. Ralph, their leader, sets up a democratic procedure by which each boy's opinion can be heard: "He who holds the Conch holds the floor." The boys eagerly accept this rule of free speech and, through it, agree that their only hope of getting off the island lies in keeping a fire burning as a way of signaling any ships that might be passing in the distance. As they ready the fire, however, the ominous forces of darkness set in and take control. Piggy, an overweight misfit who represents the voice of reason in the group, breaks his spectacles and becomes the object of ridicule. Ralph's authority is questioned. Savagery and brute force take over in the persons of Jack and Roger, who cover themselves with paint and go out with a few others in search of meat. Their killing of a wild sow awakens the savage instincts of their "tribe," as they like to call themselves. Soaked in the blood of their kill, they gut their prey and stick its decaying head on a pole in the ground, dubbing it, "The Lord of the Flies." The savagery in their veins has now risen close to their skin. The cry of the hunters calls for more blood to flow from the thrusts of their makeshift spears. When they set out to steal some fire to cook their meat with,

the carnage moves from bad to worse. Piggy is thrown off a cliff
while holding the Conch. His head splits open when it hits a rock
on impact. Ralph is severely wounded and forced into hiding. Jack
proclaims himself, "Chief." The others have no choice but to
comply. The rule of chaos would have set in even further were it not
for the fact that smoke from the fire set earlier by Ralph was finally
sighted by a passing British cruiser. The boys are rescued, but they
have lost their innocence. "The Lord of the Flies," a translation of
the Greek word "Beelzebub" (i.e., Satan), has made sure of that.

The Abolition of Man

Golding's novel portrays the shadow side of human nature,
the beast within us who is capable of the most heinous of crimes.
This theme comes through most clearly in a discussion which the
Lord of the Flies has with Simon, the group's wary visionary:

> "What are you doing out here all alone? Aren't you afraid
> of me?"
> Simon shook.
> "There isn't anyone to help you. Only me.
> And I'm the Beast."
> Simon's mouth labored, brought forth audible words.
> "Pig's head on a stick."
> "Fancy thinking the Beast was something you could hunt
> and kill!" said the head. For a moment or two the forest and
> all the other dimly appreciated places echoed with the
> parody of laughter. "You knew, didn't you? I'm part of you?
> Close, close, close! I'm the reason why it's no go? Why
> things are what they are?"[1]

---

[1] William Golding, *The Lord of the Flies* (New York, Perigee Books, 1954), 143.

Things are what they are because of the potential savagery that can erupt at any moment from the deepest recesses of the human heart. The "Lord of the Flies," the beast within, original sin — call it what you will — the outcome is always the same.

C.S. Lewis states the same raw truth in a slightly different way. In his popular ethical treatise, *The Abolition of Man*, he talks about the potential each of us has for good and for evil. In the moral arena of life, we all have a built-in capacity to transcend ourselves or to abolish ourselves. The choice is ours to make, and we must live with the consequences of it. We develop our moral potential when we admit our creatureliness and give to others the respect and dignity they deserve. We diminish it, however, when we deceive ourselves with godlike pretensions and treat other people as objects of scorn — "like things." If the latter holds sway, we slowly devolve into our animal nature and, in effect, cease being human: reason gives in to passion; instinct overcomes will; raw emotions blot out our deeper intuitions. We alone — and no one else — are responsible for our moral destiny. Such is the nature of human freedom.[2]

Observations

What are some of the implications of what Lewis is saying?

1. *No one enjoys being treated like an object.* We are not machines that can be turned on and off at whim. A thing is good in itself and is meant to be used by people for their own good and the good of others. A person, however, is not a thing and should not be treated as such —even if it be for what appears to be a noble and worthy cause. To manipulate another person — the way you would, say, a can opener, a screw driver or pocketknife — is to show a great

---

[2] C.S. Lewis, *The Abolition of Man* (New York: The Macmillan Co., 1947), 77.

lack of respect to him or her, to God, and even to ourselves. When we take away a person's dignity, we also lose something of our own.

2. *To treat another person like an object dehumanizes each of the parties involved.* One is made to feel as if he or she doesn't really count. The other opens up a moral wound in the soul which, if left untreated, numbs the conscience and drags the person down to the level of his or her animal nature. Lewis reminds us that it is possible for an individual to become totally incapable of treating another human being with respect. When this occurs, that person has lost touch with his or her sense of compassion, one of the basic moral qualities that separates humans from animals and machines alike.

3. *We lose our sense of compassion when we allow the way we interact with things to serve as the primary model for our human relationships.* This occurs largely through a process of projection. Machines do what we tell them; they get the job done; and they don't talk back. Because so much of our lives is project-oriented and measured by the "bottom line" or end-result of our efforts, it is relatively easy for us to lose sight of the intrinsic worth of others and to treat them solely as a means of achieving a particular end. To act in this way is to cheapen the value of human life and to impoverish our own moral character.

4. *To avoid this strong dehumanizing tendency in our nature we must become aware of the vast array of relationships that constitute our social makeup.* As human beings, we have the capacity to interact with and develop a relationship with God, with other people (both individually and in groups), with ourselves, our environment (animals, plants, inanimate objects), and so on. Each of these relationships is unique and should be understood and dealt with on its own terms. It would be a mistake to allow any one of them to infringe on the boundaries of the others. Just as we should not treat things as if they were gods (a mark of idolatry), so too must we avoid treating other people like things (a mark of disrespect).

5. *One of the best ways of keeping a person's dignity foremost in*

our mind is to try to imagine ourselves in his or her place. To walk in another's shoes does wonders for a person's humanity. Asking ourselves how another person might think, feel, and react in a particular situation reminds us that he or she is not really all that different from ourselves and deserves to be treated with dignity and respect. "Treat others the way you would have them treat you" (Mt 7:12). After nearly two thousand years, this well-known Gospel adage — the so-called Golden Rule — has yet to be improved upon.

6. *Unfortunately, it also has rarely been put into practice — at least not on a large scale.* The pages of human history contain innumerable tales of man's inhumanity to man. War, forced starvation, serial murders, mass executions — the beast within us has already filled countless graves with the corpses of innocent men, women, and children. Many more have simply been left to rot from the heat of the blazing sun. By most counts, the abolition of man of which Lewis speaks is already well under way. To many, there seems little that can be done to turn the tide.

The Adulterous Woman

A brief comparison of two similar situations involving women caught in adultery may shed some light on just how close our savage instincts lie beneath the surface of our skin and what can be done to tame them or, at least, keep them in check.

The first comes from Nikos Kazantzakis' famous novel, *Zorba the Greek*, the story of a feisty, wanderlust Cretan who embraces the tragedies and joys he encounters as part of the flowing rhythm of life's great cosmic dance. In one scene, a widow of the village known for her numerous love affairs, is ostracized by the entire village for daring to enter the church on Easter Sunday: "'Wretch! Slut! Murderess!' The voices cried. 'And she's got the cheek to show herself here! She's disgraced the village!'" Surrounded by her assailants, the poor woman is forced to her knees as she looks for a means of escape. Zorba intervenes on her behalf by giving Manola-kas, one of her many angry male attackers, a terrible blow in the lower part of the abdomen, thrusting him to the ground, taking away his knife, and finally walking toward the churchyard door in order to lead the startled woman away. The action continues:

> The widow stood up; she gathered all her strength together in order to rush forward. But she did not have the time. Like a falcon, old Mavrandoni threw himself on her, knocked her over, wound her long black hair three times round his arm and with a single blow of his knife cut off her head.
> "I take the responsibility for this sin!" he cried, and threw the victim's head on the doorstep of the church. Then he crossed himself.[3]

The fact that this cold-blooded murder takes place at a time of celebration, "when the paschal dance was at its height," under-scores how swiftly our brutal, savage instincts can erupt from the human heart. "A widow's head on the doorstep of the church." "A pig's head on a stick." The Lord of the Flies has numerous earthly manifestations.

The second example comes from chapter 8 of John's Gospel and relates the story of the woman caught in adultery (Jn 8:3-11). Led out by the scribes and Pharisees, this woman is forced to stand in front of everyone and made to hear the prescription of the Mosaic Law which calls for death by stoning. Asked for his opinion in the matter (probably in an attempt to trip him up), Jesus bends to the ground and writes something in the dirt with his finger. When they persist, he slowly straightens up and in one wonderful

---

[3] Nikos Kazantzakis, *Zorba the Greek*, trans. Carl Wildman (New York: Simon and Schuster, 1952), 246-47.

dramatic moment says: "Let the one among you who has no sin be the first to cast a stone at her." He then bends to the ground a second time and resumes writing in the dirt. One by one, the people drift away, beginning with the elders of the community. When only Jesus and the woman remain, he asks her: "Where did they all disappear to? Has no one condemned you?" "No one, sir," she answers. "Nor do I condemn you," Jesus responds. "You may go, but from now on avoid this sin."

Two similar situations; two completely different outcomes. Each woman is alone and has committed a serious crime in the eyes of the community. The demand for blood is strong: knives are drawn against one; stones raised against the other. In each instance, savage instincts rise to the surface and can sway the volatile crowd either way. Why does Jesus succeed and Zorba fail? Were their approaches really that very different? The similarities and differences between them make for interesting comment.

Both protagonists value the lives of the women they are defending above the crimes these women have committed and the demands for vengeance prescribed by the Law of Moses (as in the case of Jesus) or the unwritten village traditions of the island of Crete (as in the case of Zorba). Both men are very different: Zorba comes close to being an avowed hedonist; Jesus is a prophet and holy man. Despite their different characters and philosophies of life, both agree on the sacredness of human life and the importance of treating individuals —even the outcast — with dignity and respect. Each tries to preserve life in his own way: Zorba with his hands and fists; Jesus with carefully chosen words.

The difference in the outcome of these two very similar situations lies in the way their varying methods affect the women's angry accusers. By resorting to force, Zorba feeds the fury of the raging mob and possibly provokes old Mavrandoni to wield his knife the way he does. His noble intentions make a bad situation worse: violence feeds upon violence; rage upon rage. Manolakas'

loss to Zorba sends old Mavrandoni over the edge. The widow pays
for this with her life. Jesus, by way of contrast, uses not force but
words in his attempt to tame the angry crowd. By inviting the one
without sin to cast the first stone, he forces his hearers to put
themselves in the place of the sinner. By having them examine
their own lives, he removes the poor woman from the center of
attention and manages to diffuse the anger of the moment. Jesus, it
would seem, has chosen the better path. He makes others aware of
the darkness in their own lives, thus enabling them to walk in the
footsteps of the accused. He treats the poor woman with dignity,
condemning the sin and not the sinner, and manages to keep her
alive in the process. Zorba, the perennial hedonist, condemns
neither, and fails in his effort to keep the widow alive.

The Way of Jesus

Left to our own resources, none of us would be able to tame the
raging beast that prowls deep in the recesses of our hearts. Such an
enemy is too strong, too savage, too cruel for our feeble wills to
handle. It knows exactly when and how to take advantage of our
shabby defenses — and it relishes in the kill. The wisdom of Jesus
tells us that the only way to subdue it is to refuse to play its game,
to offset its hungry aggression with our own brokenness and
vulnerability. Others, besides Jesus, have also recognized this
timeless truth: Mahatma Gandhi and Martin Luther King, to name
just two outstanding examples. These courageous men from vastly
different religious and cultural backgrounds learned from hard
experience that the one thing the beast cannot overcome is the
determined path of nonresistance. The violence unleashed by the
Lord of the Flies may be checked or contained for a time by a
proportionate use of violence. It can be conquered, however, only
by refusing to participate in the vicious spiral of violence that it has

used as a means to wreak havoc on humanity ever since the dawn of time. Gandhi, King, and, of course, Jesus were determined to halt its unchecked progress through the pages of human history. They decided to draw the line in their own personal lives and, in doing so, inspired many others to follow in their footsteps.

The way of Jesus reached its climax in his passion and death on the cross. He did not defend himself; he offered no resistance to his accusers. He turned his cheek, accepted the fate of a common criminal, and bid others not to weep for him. The courage with which he faced his death gives eloquent testimony to his noble stature. This innocent man took death itself by surprise when he received all the fury of the world's inner rage with kindness and a forgiving word: "Father, forgive them; they know not what they are doing" (Lk 23:34). Death, at that moment, would lose its power over him. Its sting could no longer harm him.

The death and resurrection of Jesus dealt a mortal blow to the beast that prowls close beneath the surface of humanity's skin. Given a wound from which it could not recover, it now lashes out like a desperate animal with no place to hide. It senses its approaching death, however, and rages even more over the lonely certainty of its fate. The outcome of the story is clear: the time will come when the Lord of the Flies will no longer feed off the emotions of the human heart. Its days are numbered; its sun must set. The way of the Lord Jesus will prevail.

Conclusion

I have never killed or even witnessed the killing of another human being. Given the recent increase of violence in American society, particularly in our cities, I count myself particularly lucky. I have been fortunate enough this far in my life not to be in the wrong place at the wrong time — and I honestly hope it stays that way. Nonetheless, I am deeply saddened (and sometimes down-right depressed) to hear each night on the evening news of the horrible lack of respect for human life that pervades our culture. Murders, rapes, manslaughter, extortion, war: a short glance at the morning papers makes one wonder what has gone wrong with the world we live in. Is there no end to the violence? Are we to assume that this is the way it was meant to be? Are we to allow the shadow side of our natures to take complete control of our lives?

When I read about the people who perpetuate the violence, I ask myself: What is it that makes them do what they do? Can't they control the pain and suffering they inflict? Do they feel no remorse? Are they really any different from anyone else? Are they any different from me? I have pondered this last question for a long time and have been unable to reach a definitive answer. I do know, however, that the beast within me is still alive, that it breaks through my guard from time to time, and that it is capable of almost anything. I also know of its presence within me (many do not) and am conscious of what it can do and not do. More importantly, I know that the long shadow it casts within me can and will completely disappear once the noonday sun burns brightly in my soul and lightens every passageway of my stony heart.

I should be grateful that the beast within me never got far beyond filling dead sparrows full of lead with a pellet gun. It certainly is still capable of it. Others in that group on that brisk Saturday morning so long, long ago were not so fortunate — at least, so I am told. "Pig's head on a stick." "Woman's head on the doorstep of a church." "Dead man on a cross." Down to this very day, the wanton spiral of violence continues. The Lord of the Flies still thirsts for blood and knows precisely where, when, and how to find it. The only way to deal with it is to face it, refuse to play its game, and to call upon and follow the way of the Lord Jesus.

Book v

Loss and Gain

The newspaper said I was the runaway favorite in the mile for the county high school championships. My coach took it for granted I would win. I was trying to prove them both right as I entered the final turn with a small but respectable lead. The crowd in the stands was cheering me on. My teammates on the infield were shouting at the top of their lungs. Everyone's attention was focused on me. Victory was almost within reach, a mere 200 yards away. I could almost taste it — almost, but not quite. For some reason, I wasn't as strong as I normally am at this point in a race. Something was wrong. Maybe I shouldn't have gone out so fast. Maybe I should have let someone else do all the work rather than extend myself the way I did earlier on. Now, I was paying for it.

I could hear another runner not far behind. He was beginning to close the gap. "I got to hold on! I got to hold on!" I told myself. The crowd sensed that I was in trouble and started yelling even louder. My teammates were frantic. I stretched out my legs a little bit more in order to pick up the pace; they felt like lead. My heart was pounding wildly in my chest; it was getting harder and harder for me to breathe. "Come on! Just a little bit more!" My coach yelled. "Move your arms! Move your arms!" I broke out onto the straight-away, and I could see the finish line about 100 yards away.

It was no use: my stomach began tightening up; my neck muscles stiffened; I was pulling myself back rather than leaning my body forward. Worse yet, I took a quick look behind me to see how far back the others were. Before I knew it a runner from a rival school was right on my shoulder. He tried to overtake me, but I refused to give in. He surged a second time, and I still managed to hold him off. He got me on the third try, just thirty yards from the finish. I was dead. I was losing the race and now could do nothing about it. It had all come down to these last few seconds — which seemed to take forever. Rigor mortis was setting in. He now had a couple of strides on me. I watched him cross the finish line. Two or three others whizzed by me just a few yards from the finish. I crossed the line and collapsed onto the track. When I got to my knees, I buried my face in my hands. I didn't even place. I had let everybody down. I was disgusted with myself.

The Measure of One's Worth

Sooner or later everyone has to deal with failure. In my case, it happened on a tartan track on an overcast day during the Spring of my senior year in high school. I lost the mile in the county championships, a race just about everyone I knew — my coach, my teammates, my friends, my family — was depending on me to win. Not doing so devastated me at the time and gave me a painful memory that would haunt me for years to come.

The standards we use to measure success or failure are very personal. What one individual considers a success may have very little significance to another. Failure for one might be viewed as the complete opposite by another. For me, it wasn't so much losing the race that had made me feel like a complete and utter failure. By that time, I had won and lost enough races to believe the old harrier's adage, "Not everyone can win; somebody has to come in second;

and it's better than coming in last!" Nor was it the expectations of my friends and family that made me feel that way. They, in fact, were very supportive of me in my defeat and went out of their way to let me know they were there for me. It wasn't even the embarrassment of losing before such a big crowd. I had had my time in the limelight and would experience other such moments in life. When I think about it, I would have to say that the extreme sense of failure had come because, for some reason or other, I had convinced myself that winning that particular race on that particular day was the measure of my own self-worth. Just how I let myself get into that frame of mind, I don't think I'll ever know.

Identifying our self-worth with some external accomplishment is a particularly common form of self-deception. It usually happens when we project our ego onto some external object or activity and become so attached to it that we cannot conceive of life without it. When this occurs, the boundaries of our concept of the self become blurred: something external to the self becomes so intimately bound up with it that it is difficult to determine just where one ends and the other begins. If, for whatever reason, the two become separated (or never attained, as in my case), a person's sense of self-worth can become totally deflated. In my situation, winning the mile in the county championships had become so much a part of my self-image that losing it made me feel like a stranger to myself. It would take quite some time before I understood what was going on.

Coping with Failure

People deal with failure in a variety of ways (some more effectively than others). As with many things in life, a good number of these are spontaneous gut or emotional reactions rather than carefully reasoned responses to the situation. A brief description of three of the more common means of coping with failure may prove useful to our discussion.

1. *For some people, the prospect of failure is so unacceptable that they deny its ever having taken place.* To accomplish this feat, they make up a story about "what really happened" and convince themselves of its historical truth. When this sort of behavior touches the moral sphere, people either consciously suppress their experience or, as in the case of very traumatic events, repress their memory of it into the depths of their unconscious. Neither is an effective way of dealing with moral failure and its accompanying guilt. Sooner or later, the memory will rise to the surface and insist on being dealt with on its own terms. The results can be devastating. A typical example of someone who is unwilling to take responsibility for his moral failure is the Rev. Mr. Dimmesdale of Nathaniel Hawthorne's *The Scarlet Letter*. For years he conceals the fact that he has had a child out of wedlock with Hester Prynne, a young woman from his parish who bears her community's scorn by being made to wear the embroidered mark of an adulteress on her chest. By refusing to accept responsibility for his crime, this Puritan pastor of 17th-century Salem allows his guilt to fester inside until it literally cuts the letter "A" into his chest from within: "With a convulsive motion, he tore away the ministerial band from before his breast. It was revealed! But it were irreverent to describe that revelation."[1] Dimmesdale's unwillingness to face up to his sin compounds an already difficult situation and precipitates his early death. Only at the very end of his life does he realize what he has done and confess the error of his ways.

2. *On the other extreme, some people use failure as an instrument of defiance.* They not only invite it, but actively seek it out. In such a situation, the person in question is usually under a lot of stress. He or she is so controlled by another party that the only way of getting

---

[1] Nathaniel Hawthorne, *The Scarlet Letter* (New York: Harper & Row, 1965), 226.

even is to derail a project which the controlling party takes pride in. Thus, a child fails at school as a way of getting back at an abusive parent. A man turns to drink as a way of hurting his nagging wife. A prisoner sabotages an inspection of his cell block so that the guards immediately over him lose points. A classic example of the use of failure as a form of defiance is the youthful narrator and main character of Alan Sillitoe's *The Loneliness of the Long-Distance Runner*, who deliberately slows down and loses a cross-country race for Borstol, the British penitentiary where he is an inmate and for which he is running, just to embarrass the warden. His thoughts during the race express it best:

> I'm not going to win because the only way I'd see I came in first would be if winning meant that I was going to escape the coppers after doing the biggest bank job of my life, but winning means the exact opposite, no matter how they try to kill or kid me, means running into their white-gloved wall-barred hands and grinning mugs and staying there for the rest of my natural long life of stone-breaking anyway, but stone-breaking in the way I want to do it and not in the way they tell me.[2]

As necessary as it may seem at the time, using failure as an instrument of defiance does precious little to improve one's lot in life. When it's all over and done with, the same situation remains and may even be worse: the abuse increases; the nagging goes on; the guards find a way of getting back; the warden is still in control. Such an act of desperation normally offers little hope of real success and tends to do nothing but perpetuate the downward spiral of failure in a person's life.

---

[2] Alan Sillitoe, *The Loneliness of the Long-Distance Runner* (New York: Signet, 1959), 38-39.

3. *Others view failure as a painful, but nonetheless necessary part of the fabric of life.* These people do not go out of their way searching for failure; they would much prefer to avoid the pain and frustration that it brings; they certainly are not overjoyed when it finally comes their way — as it inevitably does. When failure touches their lives, they accept it for what it is, embrace it as a momentary glimpse of the death they know they will one day endure, and experience a release from the secondary concerns which clutter their lives and have, up until this point, given them a false sense of security. Failure gives them back their sense of perspective. They are able, once again, to see what really matters in life. They become grateful (in fact, overjoyed) for the gift of life and, despite their pain and deep feeling of loss, glory in the joy of the present moment. The two main characters of Nikos Kazantzakis' *Zorba the Greek* fit this description very well. Zorba and his timid boss have invested a great deal of time, money, and effort in a logging business which involves constructing a huge cable system that will enable them to transport the great pine trunks from the top of a steep mountain down to the sea. Their hopes of prosperity come to nil when the entire structure collapses on the first try. Stunned by the immensity of their loss, they sit on the beach utterly bewildered and with absolutely nothing to say. After the initial shock, they recognize the absurdity of it all:

> We drank and finished off the sheep, and the world was somehow lighter — the sea looked happy, the earth swayed like the deck of a ship, two gulls walked across the pebbles chattering together like human beings.
> I stood up.
> "Come on, Zorba," I cried, "teach me to dance!"
> Zorba leaped to his feet, his face sparkling.
> "To dance, boss? To dance? Fine! Come on!"
> "Off we go then, Zorba! My life has changed! Let's have it!"

"To start with I'll teach you the *Zéimbékiko*. It's a wild,
military dance; we always danced it when I was a *comitadji*,
before go into battle."
He took off his shoes and purple socks and kept on only his
shirt. But he was still too hot and removed that as well.
"Watch my feet, boss," he enjoined me. "Watch!"
He put out his foot, touched the ground lightly with his
toes, then pointed the other foot; the steps were mingled
violently, joyously, the ground reverberated like a drum.[3]

Zorba and his boss celebrate life in the midst of their misfortunes.
They find in their failed business venture an opportunity to let out
their pent up tensions and to reaffirm the wonder of simply being
alive. Their failure has given them deeper insight into the mystery
of life itself; they show their gratitude by engaging in the dance of
their lives.

Despair and Hope

Denial, defiance, and laughter are fairly common ways in
which very ordinary people cope with the reality of failure in their
lives. While the first two are very harmful to the soul, the third is
a much healthier response to the adversities of life. Even it,
however, can be harmful, especially when failure concerns the
moral sphere of life and inflicts serious harm on others (ask any
child who has been ridiculed by his or her peers for making a
mistake). Our list, however, is not yet exhausted. Nothing has yet
been said of despair and hope as possible ways of coping with (or
copping out of) failure. The apostles Judas and Peter, two well-

---

[3] Nikos Kazantzakis, *Zorba the Greek*, trans. Carl Wildman (New York: Simon and
Schuster, 1952), 290.

known New Testament figures, provide some valuable insights into these responses.

Judas, the apostle who betrayed Christ for thirty pieces of silver, is a textbook example of someone who faces his failure and is overwhelmed by what he sees. Without going into any of the popular theories about why he did what he did, the Gospels make it clear that he regretted his action, tried to give back the money he had received (and was refused), then flung the money into the temple, hung himself, and was buried in a potter's field (Mt 27:3-10). The Acts of the Apostles describes a similar sequence of events: "That individual bought a piece of land with his unjust gains, and fell headlong upon it. His body burst wide open, all his entrails spilling out" (Ac 1:18). The small discrepancies in the details do not discredit the conclusion that Judas, in all likelihood, committed suicide out of despair. Having betrayed his Master, he regretted his action and could not go on living with the weight of that failure on his conscience. In this frame of mind, death seemed a less painful choice than life. By giving in to his despair, Judas compounded his sin even more: by killing himself, he believed he was beyond the sphere of God's forgiveness and thus betrayed Christ a second time.

The apostle Peter is a New Testament figure who deals with failure in a much healthier way. The story of his cowardly denial of Christ has been recounted for centuries and thus passed on from one generation of Christians to the next. Although the details differ slightly, the general outlines of his denials are preserved by all four evangelists. Motivated by fear for his own well-being, he disowns his Master not once, but several times! Jesus himself had predicted that he would do so, and Peter is ashamed and brought to tears when he realizes that his Master's words have actually come to pass. But the story does not end there: the light of Christ dispels all darkness; Peter steps out of the shadows of denial and into the

light of God's mercy. Rather than giving in to despair, he owns up
to his shortcomings and repents. He stays with the small circle of
Jesus' followers and remains steadfast in his hope that he can and
will receive forgiveness. The results are staggering. Peter's denials
are completely reversed. He who denied Christ becomes one of the
first to proclaim his resurrection. He who was motivated by fear now
sees the strength of heartfelt compassion. His uncompromising
affirmation of faith makes him one of the pillars of the first
Christian community.

Judas and Peter respond to their failures very differently: one
gives in to despair and takes his life with his own hands; the other
lives in hope and places his life in the forgiving hands of Christ. As
apostles, both men are close followers of Christ: they number
among his most intimate friends; they accompany him throughout
his public ministry; they hear the same teaching; they witness the
same miracles. Judas' betrayal is an open denial of Christ; Peter's
denial, an implicit betrayal of him. Why do their lives have such
different outcomes? Perhaps the line separating hope from despair
is much thinner than previously thought.

Running the Good Race

A while back, when I was in one of my poetic moods, I wrote
a short little rhyme about the variety of responses I am capable of
in any given situation. If my memory serves me correctly, it went
something like this:

> Multitudes of men live their lives inside of me!
> I think of them not as a crowd, but as community!
> Each one of them contributes (some a little; some a lot)
> In making me the man I am, and not the man I'm not!

Putting the merits of the poem aside (a William Shakespeare I obviously am not), the basic insight I was trying to convey was that I, like most people, am besieged by many interior voices that constantly compete for my attention and seek to influence my decisions. These voices do not exist in isolation from each other, as they would in someone with a personality disorder such as a split personality or schizophrenia. Rather, they enter into dialogue with one another and create an internal and intensely personal discourse that ultimately persuades me to follow one particular course of action over another. Just which voice I am apt to follow depends on many factors: the mood I am in, the surrounding circumstances, the advice of others, past experience, the merits of the arguments themselves — to name just a few. If I give each voice an adequate hearing, the proper course of action eventually makes itself clear. That is not to say that I always follow what I discern to be true. Some of the voices have the potential for violence; others are outright destructive. At a given moment, any one of them can hold a powerful sway over my emotions and force me to act against my better judgment.

What has all of this to do with failure? Quite a bit. Repression, defiance, laughter, despair, and hope are some of the competing voices that condition my own behavior in moments of defeat. In particularly stressful situations, any one (or mixture) of them can rise to the surface and command my attention. The Rev. Mr. Dimmesdale, the nameless long-distance runner, Zorba, Judas, Peter all dwell within me (some more than others) and are capable of persuading me, at one time or another, to follow their various and divergent leads. I would like to believe that Peter and Zorba influence me more than the other three figures on my short (and only representative) list. I would not be honest, however, if I did not admit that the others have had their fair share of influence — something of which I am not very proud. Strangely enough, the knowledge of what I am capable of doing — ranging from good to bad to ugly — increases my awareness of my own shortcomings and enables me to be more sensitive to the failings of others. Such a sensitivity helps me in the only race that really matters.

I have returned to the image of running, the metaphor with which I began this chapter, mainly because it is used so frequently by St. Paul as a way of bringing a sense of proportion both to our failures and our successes in life (e.g., Gal 2:2; Ph 2:16, 3:12-14; 2 Tm 4:7; Heb 12:1). In one place, he writes:

> You know that while all the runners in the stadium take part in the race, the award goes to one man. In that case, run so as to win! Athletes deny themselves all sorts of things. They do this to win a crown of leaves that withers, but we a crown that is imperishable. I do not run like a man who loses sight of the finish line. I do not fight as if I were shadowboxing. What I do is discipline my own body and master it, for fear that after having preached to others I myself should be rejected (1 Cor 9:24-27).

Paul, who elsewhere describes himself as divided within (Rm 7:13-25), is fearful of losing his soul. He wonders if, despite all his preaching and missionary efforts, God will still reject him as unworthy of the redemption wrought in Christ. Since no one knows with certitude whether he or she will be saved, even the greatest of apostles must be careful not to presume too much of God. When viewed in this light, a share in Christ's victory over death is the one and only prize worth living (and dying) for; all other honors either won or lost are of secondary importance. Paul likens himself to a spiritual athlete, who runs to win the one crown that will neither wither nor fade. Everything else in life counts for very little and must be considered as such. To do otherwise (i.e., to place a transitory treasure as the ultimate measure of one's worth) is to fail at the one thing that really matters. Jesus himself says it best: "What

gain, then, is it for a man to win the whole world and ruin his life?"
(Mk 8:36).

Conclusion

Sooner or later, each of us faces failure of one sort or another.
We come up against our own limitations. We fall short of our
expected goals. The hopes we long for never take shape. Failure is
a simple fact of life that few of us know how to avoid — at least, not
for long. When it does occur (as it inevitably does), it is important
that we learn from it and view it as an opportunity for us to gain a
deeper knowledge of ourselves and the God we love.

Failure can humble the heart and awaken us to the deeper
issues of our lives. If we are not careful, however, it can also dull our
sensitivity to the things that really matter and send us on a
downward spiral of repression, misguided anger, and betrayal. Not
only is the choice ours to make. In a certain sense, we are also made
by our choices. The true mettle of a person's character shows itself
in times of adversity. What has been written of Dimmesdale, or
Sillitoe's runner, or Zorba, or Judas, or Peter, or Paul may one day
be written of us.

One good thing came from my losing that mile race so long
ago in the high school county championships: I was given the
opportunity to consider what really mattered to me in life. That
humiliating defeat helped me to examine my values and to get a
better sense of the meaning of my own self-worth. Failure had
become an instrument of my own self-understanding. It was the
beginning of a quiet conversion experience that gradually changed
my entire outlook on life and the world around me. When viewed
in this light, that moment of defeat was probably one of the finest
moments of my life. Since the day it happened, I have never been
the same.

Book vi

The Gift of Giving

It was a big box wrapped in red paper foil and shiny gold ribbon. My eye spotted it beneath the Christmas tree the moment I entered the room. I hoped it was for me, but couldn't yet be sure. With a couple of brothers and a little sister in the family, one could never know for sure — at least not at six years old. I waited impatiently as names were read out loud and the gifts were handed out. One by one they found their intended owners. One by one they were opened and shared with others in the room. "Look at what I got Mommy!" "Daddy! Did you see this!" "I can't believe it! How did he know!" Santa was thanked a thousand times over. He must have really enjoyed the cookies and milk left behind for him on the kitchen table (we knew he had a big appetite). Or maybe he was so nice because of how good we had been during the preceding year (although we knew we really weren't). Or maybe it was just because of his kind and generous nature (there was little doubt about that). Or maybe it was even a combination of all these things (yet another possibility). In any case, I was filled with excited anticipation when my name was read out and the big red box was handed to me. I feverishly tore off the wrappings and looked inside. "What could it possibly be?" I thought to myself as I opened up what I instinctively knew would be my favorite gift. In a few seconds, the suspense turned to sheer joy and gladness as I ripped open the box and held in my hands a shiny toy trumpet. Just what I wanted — the right size and everything!

Giving and Receiving

That toy trumpet was the first gift I remember ever receiving. I'm sure there were others before it. I simply can't recall them. Whenever I think of the word "gift," a trumpet is what always comes to mind. It's probably for that reason that I always associate the giving and receiving of gifts with music.

I liked that trumpet so much that I actually brought it to school with me after the Christmas holidays to show it off to my teacher and classmates. I remember taking them by surprise with my special rendition of "Three Blind Mice" — not that I could read music or anything like that. I simply followed the numbers on the instruction sheets that came in the box. I know I made a few mistakes here and there, but it still sounded good to me. Still, I could tell I was no child prodigy. The reaction of my audience, one of feigned recognition, made me sure of that. It took four or five guesses before anyone could distinguish the notes I was playing, let alone the song. A few of my friends chuckled as I labored nervously through the notes; a few others started whispering among themselves when the teacher wasn't looking. When it was all over (the whole concert took but a couple of minutes), my teacher patted me on the head and complimented me on a job well done. I felt good about myself. True, I was a little embarrassed on account of my poor playing. But that didn't matter much to me. I knew I would get better if I just kept at it. I was proud of my trumpet; it made me feel like somebody special. That is precisely what whoever gave it to me had intended.

"Giving is better than receiving," as the old saying goes. A gift received — be it all wrapped up, or a special talent one has been born with, or a skill one has acquired through hard work and practice — is not fully received until it is shared with someone else. It sounds so trite and commonplace, but it is true — probably one of the most profound truths I have ever learned. No one ever asked me to bring my trumpet to school that day. I simply brought it. It was not enough for me to play those sour notes alone in my room or in front of my family. I wanted to share my gift with a larger audience — to show it off, yes —but also to let it shine on its own merits. Granted, a Louie Armstrong I was not (and am still not), but that is really beside the point. I was giving to others something that had been freely bestowed and gratefully received. And I was enjoying myself in the process!

Playing My Guitar

I don't want to give you the wrong impression. I never was and never will be a trumpet player — not by any definition of the word. As a matter of fact, that toy trumpet of mine lasted only a few months before I broke one of the keys and had to put it down for ever. I haven't picked up another one since (although, I must admit, I do get the urge every now and then). Even though I wasn't cut out to be a trumpeter (or a musician of any sort, for that matter), in another sense, I carry that little toy instrument around with me wherever I go. Its sour notes ring in my ears whenever I give or receive a gift. Even though it was a cheap imitation, even though I played it out of key (probably as much its fault as it was mine), even though it broke long before its time, it has become a symbol for me of what giving a gift (and receiving one) is really all about.

Only the story of my first guitar (and what happened to it) has made a deeper impression on me. There is nothing astonishing about the event itself. During my last year of college, I bought a steel string guitar with my hard earned money and was determined to learn how to play it. I did a fairly good job of it, I might add. I took time to learn all the major chords, how to strum properly and even how to finger pick. I was making good progress and even felt comfortable playing in the company of others. I was even at the point where I was beginning to learn how to read sheet music. That, I thought, would be quite an accomplishment.

When college was over, I met someone who was a much better guitar player than I, but who had no instrument to practice on — at least not at the time. Since he lived nearby, we worked out an agreement whereby he would borrow mine from time to time and teach me a few chords, strums, and finger picks in return. The arrangement worked out rather well. As I got to know him over the next couple of years, I realized that he had a gift for music that needed to be fostered. I was determined to do what I could to help him and ultimately resorted to the only option I had at the time. When circumstances were such that each of us had to go our separate ways, I said good-bye to him by giving him the gift of my guitar.

This simple gesture of friendship was one of the most difficult things I had ever done in my life. It would not be an exaggeration to say it was like losing an arm or a leg — perhaps worse. That guitar had become so much a part of me that it was hard for me to envision life without it. By giving it to my friend, I was letting go of a part of myself. In doing so, I was letting him know that I wanted him to carry a memory of me with him as he left and hoped that he would remember me from time to time when he played it. As I gave it to him, I almost couldn't believe what I was doing; it hurt so much to give it away. I knew, however, that I was doing the right thing. All things considered, it was much better for him to have it.

My friend deeply appreciated my gift, especially since he knew how much that guitar meant to me. We have stayed in touch over the years and continue to remain close. As it turns out, he decided to develop his musical talent and to pursue a career in the entertainment business. He has produced several records and now has his own recording studio. I like to think that I played some small part in his modest success story. To this day, I remain one of his biggest fans.

The Gift Behind The Gift

An old proverb summarizes this popular sentiment about giving in a few, short, easy to remember words: "It is the thought that counts." Unfortunately, the truth of this statement is so obvious that few people take it seriously anymore. Our society has become so fixated on material wealth as the accepted expression of who and what we are that we have lost our ability to appreciate the spiritual dimension of the gifts we give and receive. We are no longer able (or willing) to recognize the gift behind the gift.

Probably nowhere is the true spirit of giving expressed more clearly than in O. Henry's celebrated short story, "The Gift of the Magi." Set in Manhattan during the early years of the present century, it tells the story of a young couple whose love for one another is so deep that it brings them to sacrifice their most cherished possessions for the sake of the other. At the outset, the couple is described as hard working, but struggling, with little money to spare for any of the typical holiday cheer. As Christmas approaches, each one wonders privately what he or she can give to the other as a gift. The husband has nothing of any worth but a gold watch that had been his father's and grandfather's; the wife, nothing but her long, beautiful hair. As the tale unfolds, each goes off separately and sells what little he or she has in order to buy a gift for the other. The husband sells his watch in order to buy an expensive set of combs for his wife; the wife cuts her hair and sells it in order to buy a platinum fob chain for her husband's watch. In the end, the couple is much worse off materially than at the beginning: the husband has a chain without a watch; the wife has a set of combs with very little hair to take care of. From a spiritual perspective, however, they are much closer than ever before. Each realizes what the other has sacrificed in order to make the other one happy. Each recognizes the gift of self behind the actual material gift that was given. The platinum chain and the combs become symbols of their love for one another and help them to understand the true meaning of giving. Both are grateful for their gifts and together celebrate Christmas in a way they never had before.

More than anything else, O. Henry's story highlights the character of reciprocity involved in the giving and receiving of gifts. A good deal of thought goes into each present and, even though neither turns out to be very appropriate at the time, each is a true measure of the deep love they share. In one sense, neither could have given the other a better gift. Both the watch chain and the hair comb represent the uncommon degree of self-sacrifice each is willing to make for the happiness of the other.

The Giving Tree

A genuine gift involves an authentic giving of self. Such a bestowal can take place in any number of ways: through an actual material gift, through a simple exchange of words (be they written or spoken), by spending time with another, by listening to him or her, by simply being present to another person. However it is done, what is important is that the other person's interests be placed squarely before one's own. The scope of this self-giving can range anywhere from the most trivial details of life to the most dramatic. One is limited only by one's imagination and by how far one is willing to go in the act of self-giving.

The children's best seller, *The Giving Tree* by Shel Silverstein gets this message across in typical storybook fashion. It follows the life of a young boy, whose friendship with a tree brings him many blessings throughout his long, worrisome life. In his carefree youth, the tree invites him to play in her leaves, to climb in her branches, to rest in her shade, and to eat of her fruit. When he is a young man and in need of money, she invites him to gather all of her apples and sell them in the city. When he has reached maturity and has a wife and children to support, she invites him to cut down her branches and use them to build a home for his family. Years later, when he dreams of traveling to far away places, she tells him to cut down her trunk and to make a boat so that he can sail far, far away. Finally, in his old age, when he is all alone with nothing to do and with no one to talk to she invites him to sit down on her useless old stump and rest his weary bones. Throughout her life, the tree thinks of nothing else but the welfare of the boy. She is willing to sacrifice her own well-being for that of her friend — even to the point of death. Even then, she still seeks a way to comfort her friend. The final words of the story describe her feelings best: ". . . and the tree was happy."

Few stories capture the meaning of love and friendship with such depth and childlike simplicity. Few portray in so vivid a manner the extent to which some are willing to go for those they deeply care for and are concerned about. Few bring to life with such vigor the underlying sense of the well-known Gospel adage: "There is no greater love than this: to lay down one's life for one's friends" (Jn 15:13). For this reason, it would not be at all far-fetched to suggest that the story of the giving tree resembles closely the way of the cross. As Jesus himself asserts: "Whoever would save his life will lose it, but whoever loses his life for my sake will find it" (Mt 16:25).

The Gift of Jesus

Jesus' entire life may be likened to a continuous action of selfless concern for others. His gift to us involves a fourfold movement where he: (1) enters our world, (2) gives of himself completely — to the point of dying for us, (3) becomes our spiritual food and (4) source of our hope. Each of these elements says something very important about his legacy to the world and the gift of redemption he offers to each of us.

1. *"The Word was made flesh and made his dwelling among us"* (Jn 1:15). When Jesus was born, Mary laid him in a manger and wrapped him in swaddling clothes (Lk 2:7). Our Christian faith hinges on the belief that God did not stand aloof from human affairs but freely chose to become one of us and share our own experiences, thoughts, and feelings. The Word of God entered our world and lived life in all its fullness (from the womb to the tomb, as some have been wont to express it). He was under no obligation to do so. His only motivation was a love for the Father which overflowed into a love for the Father's children. In this respect, the birth of Jesus reveals the depth of God's love for each one of us. The Incarnation would have taken place even if there were only one of us left in the world for God to love.

2. *". . . he emptied himself and took the form of a slave"* (Ph 2:7). Jesus did not quickly step in and out of our world (as if only to get his feet wet). He gave himself to us completely — to the point of dying for us. A quick glance at his public ministry reveals the extent to which his life was completely oriented toward the service of others. His parables, prayers, and beatitudes, his cures and miracles, his journeys throughout Galilee and eventually to Jerusalem itself, all reveal the heart of a man who is deeply aware of the needs of others and eager to do all within his power to fill them. Jesus was most intent on treating the deep wounds in the human heart caused by sin and division. His death on the cross was his way of bringing

about such a healing. From that moment on, the stranglehold which sin and death had over the human race was broken once and for all.

3. *"Do this as a remembrance of me"* (Lk 22:19). In his final meal on earth, Jesus performed a prophetic action whose symbolism revealed the very heart of his messianic identity. Having gathered his closest disciples around him, he offered bread and wine as the symbols of the New Covenant soon to be ratified by his blood. This sacrament represents both a foreshadowing and a continuation of his sacrificial death. He has given of himself completely, to the point of dying and beyond, to the point of becoming nourishment for others. Whenever the Christian community celebrates the Eucharist, it remembers Christ's death and anticipates with joy his future coming. At the very center of the Church's life and activity, the Eucharist extends to all of humanity and applies throughout all time the effects of Christ's passion, death, and Resurrection.

4. *"If there is no resurrection of the dead, Christ himself has not been raised"* (1 Cor 15:13). Christ's Resurrection is not an isolated event with no repercussions for humanity. It points, rather, to what we ourselves have in some way already experienced in Christ and hope one day fully to become: transformed, saved, resurrected, wholly ourselves. Without the Resurrection, there is nothing to hope for: faith is worthless; life is meaningless; Christ is dead. With the Resurrection there is everything to hope for; everything to live for; indeed, everything even to die for. The Resurrection verifies the truth of all that has gone before it, i.e., the Incarnation, the Eucharist, Christ's Passion and Death. And it is the testimony of Cephas, the Twelve, James, Paul, and all the others who have experienced the Risen Lord, which verifies and makes credible the meaning of our faith. We hope because others hope on account of what they have seen and come to believe.

Taken individually, these four movements correspond to different facets of the mystery of Christ: the first, to his Incarnation;

the second, to his earthly life; the third, to his institution of the
Eucharist; the fourth, to his Resurrection. Taken as a whole, they
form a coherent statement of the nature of Christ's gift to the world:
Christ came to us in his Incarnation, gave of himself completely in
both his living and his dying, gave us in the Eucharist the nourishment of his own body and blood, and promised us in his Resurrection the life of a transformed humanity. Taken both individually
and as a whole, they provide us with a deeper insight into the
meaning of Christ's love for us. They invite us to respond accord-
ingly.

Conclusion

I have always associated gifts with the sound of music, be it the
sour notes of a shiny toy trumpet, the strong, brassy sounds of a steel
string guitar, or the low guttural voice of my own on-key (and
sometimes off-key) accompaniment. Music, to my mind, is an
appropriate metaphor for the giving and receiving of gifts. It
requires someone to write it, to play it, to hear it, and to enjoy it.
It exists not as an end in itself, but as an instrument through which
the human spirit expresses itself and hopefully discovers who and
what it is all about. The same can be said for any present that has
been genuinely given and received. The same can be said for the gift
of the Lord Jesus.

"Suddenly, there was with the angel a multitude of the
heavenly host, praising God and saying, 'Glory to God in high
heaven, peace on earth to those on whom his favor rests'" (Lk 2:13-
14). One Gospel depicts Jesus' birth as having taken place amidst
a fanfare of the heavenly host. The shepherds who witnessed it
returned praising and glorifying God after finding a child wrapped
in swaddling clothes (Lk 2:20). Another Gospel speaks of astrolo-
gers bearing gifts of gold, frankincense, and myrrh (Mt 2:11). Even

Mary, his mother, proclaims her joyful Magnificat: "My being proclaims the greatness of the Lord" (Lk 1:46). However it is depicted, the intended message is clear: Jesus is God's gift to the world. Because of this gift, the world would never be the same.

Such is the lesson of the giving tree, of which the cross (or the tree of life, however you wish to call it) is the example par excellence. The Gospel command is clear: "If a man wishes to come after me, he must deny his very self, take up his cross, and follow in my steps" (Mk 8:34). Just as Christ entered our world and gave of himself completely to the point of becoming nourishment and a source of hope for us, so we are called, both individually and as a group, to enter the various worlds of the people around us and to give ourselves to them in a manner similar to Christ's own self-offering. We are called to do this to the point that we too might become nourishment for others and a source of life-giving hope for them. This call to discipleship reveals to us the fundamental meaning of our Christian identity. It is accomplished, not by ourselves alone, but by our cooperating with Christ working in us and influencing us by the grace of his Spirit. It is, without a doubt, one of the greatest gifts in life a person can receive.

Book VII

What Happened to Him?

T
he two little boys had wandered into the empty, inner-city church just minutes before. They now stood paralyzed before the huge larger-than-life-sized crucifix that hung in the old church vestibule. Their eyes were fixed on the tortured, bloodied corpus. It must have been the first time they had ever seen a representation of Jesus' death (or even heard of him, for that matter). As I ventured to pass them, one caught sight of me from the corner of his eye. He pulled on my shirt and pointed to the sad, tormented figure saying with the utter innocence that only a child can muster: "Hey — what happened to *him?*" Even as the standard answer left my lips, a simple verse of a memorable but long-dead English poet came almost spontaneously to mind: "Thought would destroy their paradise. No more; — where ignorance is bliss 'Tis folly to be wise."[1] I felt embarrassed.

A Child's Vision

If only with each new day we could experience the cross as if for the first time — through the eyes of our distant childhood. If

---

[1] Thomas Gray, "Ode on a Distant Prospect of Eton College," in *Immortal Poems of the English Language*, ed. Oscar Williams (New York: Washington Square Press, 1952), 193.

such were the case, our questions (I dare say) would be profoundly simple, refreshingly spontaneous, and probably annoyingly end-less. Through the eyes of our inquisitive (yet often neglected) inner child perhaps we might uncover insights long since forgotten, buried beneath the intellectual debris of our highly elaborated (yet often stifling) rational sophistication. Perhaps by befriending the child within us we could find the way toward our long sought after spiritual rebirth (Jn 3:5). Perhaps we could come to understand more deeply the childlike acceptance of God's kingdom that Jesus asks of us all (Mk 10:15). Perhaps — perhaps not.

Just how good a thing is it to put even the most innocuous of childlike questions to the steadfast tenets of our faith? Perhaps the shadow side of us would react against (and possibly even abuse) what we uncover. Perhaps we would feel threatened if we delve too deeply. Perhaps we would become disillusioned and emerge even more cynical than many of us already are. Perhaps we should take the advice of the incorrigible university professor who said: "To search in order to find the world's beginning and end is a disease ... The normal person lives, struggles, experiences joy and sorrow, gets married, has children, and does not waste his time asking whence, wither and why."[2] Perhaps we should just live our lives and not concern ourselves with what it's all about. Perhaps to do otherwise would be nothing but a waste of time. Will we ever find a satisfactory answer to any of our really significant questions? I have spent most of my life asking questions, and I must honestly admit: I wonder — I sometimes wonder. Or maybe we are just not asking the right kind of questions.

---

[2] Nikos Kazantzakis, *Report to Greco*, trans. P.A. Bien (New York: Simon and Schuster, Inc., 1965), 341.

George's Story

One of the most important things I have learned in my life I got not from a teacher, or a book, not from going to class, or by doing research — activities of such consequence — but from visiting a 17-year-old boy in the hospital named George Kallfelz.

George was dying of lymphomatoid leukemia and had been in the hospital for a long time. When I first saw him, he seemed like a little boy in an old man's frame. He was so thin and pale. He looked undernourished, had lost a lot of weight, and nearly all of his hair. Worse yet, a strange aura of death enveloped him. Looking as though he had barely survived (or just recently succumbed to) the horrors of a Nazi concentration camp, he reminded me of death incarnate.

George knew he was very sick, and he had been told that he did not have very long to live. But that did not seem to bother him — at least not on the surface. He was more concerned with the cramps he was getting in his right leg and which, because of his lack of exercise from being bedridden for so long, simply refused to go away. He kept on rubbing and massaging it, usually to little or no avail.

I visited George many times in the upcoming weeks. His condition grew steadily worse, and he seemed to be more and more bothered by those cramps. Finally, his patience wore thin. On one particular visit, when the cramps were particularly bothersome, he went into a state of outright rage. All of the anger and denial that had been pent up in him for so many years became focused on the cramp in his right leg. He just could not understand why, after all he was going through, he had to have cramps in his leg as well. He started hitting his leg and pounding it. "Why don't you leave me alone? Why don't you go away? Why don't you leave me *alone*?" And then, in the midst of all of the raw emotion, when he sensed how futile it all was, he raised his fists to heaven and cried out: "Why is this happening to me? Why is this happening? Isn't cancer bad *enough?*" He started to cry and to sob, finally able to let everything out of his system. I felt helpless. All I could do was reach out and put my hand on his shoulder, just to let him know that someone was there. I sensed from him a hesitant and pained sense of gratitude.

That moment marked the beginning of George's long journey towards the acceptance of his approaching death. In the weeks ahead, he would continue to deal with his anger and grief and eventually discover a hidden source of peace resting deep within his heart. He died at his home in Binghamton, New York on August 6, 1983.

Questions from the Heart

George's story is not unusual. Change a few of the names and circumstances and his story could be any one of a thousand others of tragic loss and needless suffering. "The good die young," so they say. What small recompense for a life so soon deprived. Such words bring little comfort to loved ones left behind. "Why did you have to be *so good?*" I can hear them saying.

George's life and his pain touched me deeply. He taught me that the most important questions in life come not from the mind, but the heart. His "Why?" was a cry of pain. He was not looking for a neat explanation or a consistent theory that would solve all his problems. His questions sprang from his anxiety. They were complaints of the good who suffer — outcries of anger, sobs of helplessness, laments of last resort. His cries echoed the defiance of Job: "I cry to you, and you give me no answer; I stand before you, but you take no notice. You have grown cruel in your dealings with me, your hand lies on me, heavy and hostile" (Job 30:20-21).[3] I sometimes

---

[3] *The Jerusalem Bible* (Garden City, NY: Doubleday and Co., Inc., 1966).

wonder if George really died of a broken heart not for lack of love (that was certainly present in abundance), but because it could no longer physically contain the cry of his deep human anguish.

True Confessions

I have a confession to make. When I first set about putting together my thoughts for this reflection on the meaning of Jesus' suffering, George's story and, yes, even the lesson that it had taught me, were very far from my mind. One of the liabilities of academic types like myself, who shut themselves up in libraries and their studies researching the finer points of theology, is that they can gradually shut themselves off from the real questions — those of the heart — that nearly everyone has and are usually most concerned about. If we are not careful, we can all too easily avoid or refuse to face them — at least head on.

No, this reflection was originally going to be a straight-forward intellectual exercise. In answering these questions, I was going to develop the three main theories that theologians have developed over the years in order to explain the meaning of what happened to Jesus of Nazareth on the cross almost two thousand years ago: (1) ransom, (2) satisfaction, and (3) instruction or moral example. I was going to lay them out clearly, compare them, point out their strengths and weaknesses, show how they complement one another, as I have already done many times before, so many times, in fact, that I could almost do it in my sleep.

The *ransom* theory, for example, developed within the patristic tradition and was prevalent for the first thousand years of the Church's history. Evident in such thinkers as Augustine and Gregory the Great, it focuses on Jesus' statement in Mt 20:28 that he came "to give his life as a ransom for many." Jesus' death is understood as the ransom that God pays to Satan in order to release humanity from the chains of sin and death. This approach employs mythic language and sees redemption as taking place on a cosmic plane in some grand battle between the forces of Christ and those of Satan. We are nothing but passive onlookers.

The *satisfaction* theory, in contrast, was developed by Anselm of Canterbury in the late 11th-century work, the *Cur Deus homo* (1098). It rejects the model of divine ransom and focuses instead on the infinite magnitude of the sin of Adam. This theory takes Satan completely out of the picture. Jesus, the expression God's infinite compassion, dies on the cross, not to ransom us from Satan, but to satisfy the infinite demands of God's justice. Employing legal language, this theory eventually becomes the mainstay of Church teaching and remains so right up to the present. It puts humanity and God face to face. Jesus' death on the cross is understood as the way in which God's mercy satisfies the demands of God's justice. The wrath of God is quieted by his incarnate mercy.

The *instruction* (or moral) theory rejected both the ransom and satisfaction models as ridiculous. First developed by the scholastic theologian Peter Abelard and adopted centuries later by a number of the proponents of Protestant Liberalism, it insists that Jesus died on the cross not to ransom us from Satan or to satisfy God's justice, but to give us an example, i.e., to show us how to love. It uses a variety of poetic images to convey the idea that Jesus' death on the cross reveals to those who experience it the true meaning of love. Jesus' humble act of total self-surrendering love is meant to move us and evoke from us a similar response.[4]

More or less, that was going to be it. Ransom, satisfaction, instruction: three different attempts to explain the significance of Jesus' death on the cross. Oh, I would have dressed them up a little

---

[4] For an analysis of these various theories of redemption, see Gustaf Aulen, *Christus Victor: An Historical Study of the Three Main Types of the Idea of the Atonement*, trans. A.G. Herbert (New York: Macmillan Publishing Co. Inc., 1969), 143-59.

more. I would have made them seem a bit more interesting by drawing out some of their finer subtleties. But, by and large, that was pretty much going to be it. As they say in Rome, "Basta . . . finito!"

A Change of Heart

Something happened to me, however, when I first took pen to hand to write down these thoughts — and I know exactly what it was. I started thinking about George and his cry from the heart: "Why? Why? Why?" His memory, and those words in particular, began to haunt me; I still have not been able to get them out of my mind. Gradually, I came to realize that it all had to do with the task I had before me, i.e., reflecting on the significance of Jesus' suffering and the meaning of our redemption.

You see, these theories which I have just briefly outlined for you have not weathered time very well. They no longer speak to the heart —at least not my heart — and I would imagine not yours as well. Perhaps they never did. They have become brittle and stale. Today they may be intellectually pleasing to a historical theologian (like myself) who studies the rise and interplay of ideas through time but, for the most part, they have lost their emotive force — they no longer inspire or move the heart. As the saying goes, "They are nothing to die for."

Even on the intellectual level, they fail to satisfy our modern sensitivities. A recent review of Kenneth Grayston's *Dying, We Live* (New York: Oxford University Press, 1990) puts the matter quite clearly:

Why should forgiveness require the shedding of blood? . . . Indeed, it is a question that has never been satisfactorily answered. To call the crucifixion a substitute punishment, or a sacrificial death, or a ransom, is merely to raise additional questions. Why would a good and gracious God

require an innocent man to suffer and die for the forgiveness of others? Why would he demand a sacrifice? Why a
lethal ransom? . . . And as far as satisfaction goes, how can
God persuade sinners to rely on his merciful love when, all
the while, they are enduring the awful consequences of his
wrath. . . . None of these themes has explained to the
satisfaction of modern people why a death was necessary in
God's scheme of things for our sins to be forgiven.[5]

To tell you the truth, when I reflect upon these theories, I can
identify strongly with little Willie, a character in Thomas Klise's
novel, *The Last Western*. Willie is a 7-year-old Afro-Chinese-Irish-
Mexican-Indian American boy who, early on in the story, is not
allowed to receive his First Holy Communion because he refuses to
learn his catechism. Willie's mother brings him to Sister Gabriela,
his religion teacher, and the dialogue goes like this:

Willie's mother again turned to her son.
"Willie, who is Jesus?"
"The one who died on the cross."
"And why did he die on the cross?"
"Because his father made him."
"But why?" said Sister Gabriela.
"I don't know why, Sister," said Willie.
"To atone for the sins of man," Sister Gabriela said.
"Surely you can remember how often we went over that in
class."
"I remember," Willie said, "but I do not understand." He
squirmed in his chair, smiling.
"You don't have to understand, Willie," said Sister Gabriela,
"you only have to believe."
What Willie said then shocked both the sister and his
mother.

[5] W. William Anderson, "Why Was Christ's Death Necessary?" *Harvard Divinity Bulletin*
21 (no. 1, 1991-92): 19.

"I do not believe it then," he said.

The next day Willie was sent to see Father Simpson, who sometimes taught religion to the older boys and girls.[6]

Willie asks some very good questions. He goes to the heart of the matter. Why did Jesus have to die? Ransom? Satisfaction? To give us good example? None of these explanations really give a satisfactory answer. They fail to convince us. We know instinctively that his death could have been avoided and that Jesus' real reason for dying is mysteriously hidden in the mind of God, our Father. In the words of Alphonsus Liguori, Doctor of the Church and patron of confessors and moral theologians:

> It was not necessary for the Redeemer to die in order to save the world; a drop of his blood, a single tear, or prayer, was sufficient to procure salvation for all; for such a prayer, being of infinite value, should be sufficient to save not one but a thousand worlds.[7]

From Mind to Heart

To discover the significance of the mystery of Redemption in our lives, we have to look beyond the theories that our minds have concocted over the centuries. I am not suggesting that we simply ignore or discard them. No, there are elements of truth in each of them; when taken together, they give us a glimpse into the mysterious intentions of God's plan. By viewing redemption in terms of a mythic struggle between God and Satan, the ransom model focuses on the cosmic reality of *divine-human unrelation.* By

---

[6] Thomas S. Klise, *The Last Western* (Valencia, CA: Tabor Publishing, 1974), 34.

[7] Alphonsus Liguori, *Dignity and Duties of the Priest, or Selva* in *The Ascetical Works*, ed. Eugene Grimm, vol. 12 (Brooklyn, NY: Redemptorist Fathers, 1927), 26.

putting God and humanity face to face, the satisfaction model calls attention to the element of *divine-human relation*. By bringing to the fore our own internal response to the cross, the instruction (or moral) model emphasizes the redemptive aspect of *human inner relation*. More recently, by pondering the societal implications of God's redemptive justice, liberation theologians have highlighted the element of *human social relation*. I am saying that we must try to look beyond them. Of the mystery of Christ and his cross we must begin to ask questions that come not from the head (we are usually very good at that), but from the heart. Once we start doing that, we will find that the focus on Christ and his cross will shift from a concentration on sin and satisfaction and be understood more and more in light of God's response to human suffering. One theologian puts it this way:

> It is only because I can see God entering the darkness of human suffering and evil in his creation, recognizing it for what it really is, meeting it and conquering it, that I can accept a religious view of the world. Without the religious dimension, life would be senseless, and endurance of its cruelty pointless; yet without the cross it would be impossible to believe in God.[8]

Such is the case for Frances Young, the author of these words — and I would have to say for myself as well.

Someone once said: "There is a cross in God before the wood is seen on Calvary."[9] The cross of Christ is God's response to our human suffering: he is meeting us where we are and knows that we

[8] Frances Young in *The Myth of God Incarnate*, ed. John Hick (London: SCM Press, 1977), 34-35. Cited in Kenneth Leech, *Experiencing God: Theology as Spirituality* (New York: Harper and Row, Publishers, 1985), 299-300.

[9] Horace Bushnell, *The Vicarious Sacrifice* (1866), 35-36. Cited in Leech, *Experiencing God*, 301.

really do not want to know all the reasons. Besides, even if we could fully understand every reason in the mind of God, would it ever ease any of our pain? Would my friend George's suffering have been any less? What we want from God is compassion; we want him to touch our hearts, to suffer with us, to die with us — and so he does.

Nikos Kazantzakis, in his quasi-autobiographical novel, *Report to Greco*, the last book written before his death in 1957, captures this contemporary experience of Christ and his cross very well. He writes:

> In order to mount to the Cross, the summit of sacrifice, and to God, the summit of the Spirit, Christ passed through all the stages which the man who struggles passes through. All — and that is why His suffering is so familiar to us; that is why we pity Him, and why His final victory seems to us so much our own future victory. That part of Christ's nature which was profoundly human helps us to understand Him and to love Him and to pursue His Passion as though it were our own. If he had not within Him this warm human element, He would never be able to touch our hearts with such assurance and tenderness; He would not be able to become a model for our lives. We struggle, we see Him struggle also, and we find strength. We see that we are not all alone in the world. He is fighting on our side.[10]

From Heart to God

Why a Redeemer? Why a Cross? I assure you, the answer will be very different depending upon whether these questions come from our head or our heart. Christ may have died to ransom us from the power of Satan, or to satisfy God's justice for Adam's sin, or to

---

[10] Kazantzakis, *Report to Greco*, 278.

teach us the ways of virtue. He may have come for some mysterious combination of all of these things, which we cannot fully understand, and which is entirely known to the mind of God alone. I prefer to believe that he came simply to be with us — to be beside us as we struggle, to suffer as we suffer, to carry the cross that we ourselves will one day hang from. Jesus has gone before us. He has gone through it all and is right now beside us. This may not be very satisfying intellectually. There is no overarching theory that makes sense out of everything. It leaves a lot of questions unanswered. It too fails to satisfy the mind, but it makes perfect sense to the heart — and to anyone who has ever been in love.

"Why is this happening? Why is this happening? Isn't cancer bad enough?" "Eloi, Eloi, lama sabachthani? My God, my God, why have you forsaken me?" (Mk 15:34). Jesus was very close to my friend George during those last days of his life. He was closer than I or his parents or relatives or any of his friends could ever come. That seems to be the way it was meant to be. This I know: Jesus died on the cross so that he could be with George in that close intimate way: to suffer with him, to bleed with him, to cry with him, to share his heart with him and, yes, to point to the end of his suffering, to a place beyond, to keep alive the hope, in the midst of all the darkness, that his pain would soon be transformed by the tender embrace of God's enduring love.

Book VIII

Welcoming the Stranger

An unfamiliar figure emerges from the crowd and stalks the periphery of our small, intimate gathering. Our eyes grow weary surveying his slow, careful movements. His nameless face evokes little recognition; his lack of words conceals his tongue and place of origin. His presence poses a threat; his intentions are obscure. We feel self-conscious and ill-at-ease, uncertain about how to react. Who is this outsider? How dare he disturb the quiet peace of our inner circle! What could he possibly want from us? Our own uneasiness breaks the uncomfortable silence. Someone mouths a few words of nervous welcome. The circle slowly opens and expands; all eyes are focused on this stranger in our midst. Greetings are exchanged; stories told; food and drink shared. Our welcome is a way of befriending him. He accepts and returns our hesitant gestures of kindness. Somehow, his eyes now seem strangely familiar.

Welcoming the Stranger

Showing hospitality to strangers is a near universal characteristic of human culture. According to ancient sagas, Celtic kings or chieftains were obliged to offer food and lodging to every passing stranger — with no questions asked. In Arab lands, the sharing of food made the guest a temporary family member, conferring on him or her a number of rights and privileges — as well as obligations. To the Greeks and Romans, it was one of the main indications of a cultured civilization, marking the difference between a barbarian and a civilized person. The Jewish faith has its own rich tradition of showing hospitality to strangers. Melchizedek blesses Abram at Salem and invites him to partake in a ritual sharing of bread and wine (Gn 14:17-24). Abraham displays extraordinary kindness at Mamre to the messengers of Yahweh, who reciprocates with the promise of a son for his barren wife Sarah (Gn 18:1-15). The Deuteronomist provides his readers with a memorable reminder of the Exodus experience: "So you too must befriend the alien, for you were once aliens yourselves in the land of Egypt" (Dt 10:19). The Christian tradition goes even further when it affirms the close link between love of God and neighbor, especially those unknown to us and who have even hurt us. Gospel pericopes such as the call of Levi (Mk 2:13-17), the conversion of Zacchaeus (Lk 19:1-10), and the cure of the blind Bartimaeus (Mk 10:46-52) reveal Jesus' concern for those on the social periphery. Parables like "The Good Samaritan" (Lk 10:29-37) and "The Prodigal Son" (Lk 15:11-32) were composed by someone especially sensitive to the stranger and outcast in our midst. And then there are the words of Matthew's Gospel: "I was hungry and you gave me food, I was thirsty and you gave me drink. *I was a stranger and you made me welcome*" (Mt 25:35-37).

But who are the strangers in our midst? Where and how far are we to search for them? Are we to be content with the word's most obvious meaning, i.e., those persons with whom we are unacquainted and who remain unknown to us? Or should we be more attuned to a variety of possible meanings that will take into account a wider range of relevant applications? When seriously considered, the latter possibility has much in its favor. It points to the presence of the stranger in three important areas of our lives: within, in others, in God.

The Stranger Within

Before he can enter the heart of Mordor and drop the ominous Ring that threatens the destruction of Middle-earth into the fiery crack of Mount Doom, Frodo, the hero of J.R.R. Tolkien's epic tale, *The Lord of the Rings*, must first confront his own inner darkness and lethal insecurities. This Herculean task is a challenge for all of us: the enemy or stranger within is the first (and perhaps the greatest) obstacle to true spiritual growth.

1. *Befriending Our Fears.* An authentic love of neighbor cannot exist without a prior and corresponding love of self (Lk 10:27). Our experience of self, however, is all too often one of division and inner struggle (Rm 7:15-16). We need to learn how to be comfortable with ourselves by spending time alone and befriending the stranger within. For starters, this would entail coming to terms with our innermost fears, i.e., that strange mix of common misgivings and anxieties that we share with most other people and those others that are unique to our own personal constitutions. To do so, one often must embark on a long, harrowing spiritual journey.

Dorothy, the 12-year-old heroine of *The Wizard of Oz*[1] is an example of someone who has made such an adventurous trek. On her way to meet the Wizard, the only one in Oz who supposedly knows how to get her home, she befriends three extraordinary and very colorful creatures: a scarecrow in search of a brain, a tin man without a heart, and a cowardly lion. As Dorothy's fellow travellers

---

[1] The version of *The Wizard of Oz* referred to in these paragraphs is the 1939 movie, which differs in many ways from L. Frank Baum's book first published in 1900.

on her adventure into the darkest and gloomiest part of Oz, each of these characters intervenes on her behalf at some decisive moment, demonstrating (much to his surprise) that he already has what he is looking for! The potential of each is far greater than what anyone had ever imagined.

The meaning of the fairy tale becomes clear only when one realizes that these characters are the author's creative way of rendering for the developed sensitivities of his day the classical divisions of the Platonic understanding of the soul: the rational (usually represented by a man), the consupiscible (an ox, the symbol of material productivity in classical times — depicted as a man of tin for readers of an industrial age) and the irascible (normally depicted as a lion).[2] When seen in this light, each of these characters may be understood as a unconscious projection of Dorothy's innermost fears. Like most of us, Dorothy is afraid of being thought stupid (it is interesting that the antagonist of the tale is a wicked witch who very much resembles Dorothy's austere schoolmarm back in Kansas). Like most of us, she is also afraid of showing her emotions (a dominant fear for an American audience largely formed by the stoical mores of the Protestant work ethic). Like most of us, she is also afraid of confronting her fears (just as the lion runs from his own shadow). The Wizard, who is really an old circus entrepreneur who is better at giving small doses of proverbial advice than performing extraordinary feats of magic (of which he knows very little), cannot help Dorothy because her journey is one of mind and spirit rather than physical distance. Only Dorothy can find what by all other accounts is an arduous and perilous way home. She does so eventually by simply clicking her heels and verbalizing her soul's deepest desire: "There's no place like home. There's no

---

[2] The connection between the man, the lion, and the ox with Platonic anthropology stems from the patristic allegorical tradition. See for example, Jerome's *Commentary on Ezekiel* 1:7 (*PL* 25:22).

place like home. . . ." Awaking from a seemingly endless sleep, she finds new excitement in the ordinary things of her Midwestern American life. By befriending her fears, she is able to experience those around her in a new and different light.

How do we befriend our fears? Like Dorothy, we have to travel with them; adventure with them; get close to them; tame them. Only then will we be able to tap our deeper potential and envisage the person each of us so deeply desires to become. Only then will we be able to leave them behind — as we make our way back to Kansas.

2. *Befriending Ourselves.* It is not enough, however, simply to come to terms with our fears. We must also welcome and befriend our very selves. In one of his earliest letters, the Apostle Paul bids farewell to his readers by praying that they be kept safe and blameless "spirit, soul, and body" (1 Th 5:23). Elsewhere, he uses the analogy of the body to point out the social nature of our existence in Christ (1 Cor 12:12-26). Humanity is a composite of these four anthropological levels. Since there is a spiritual, mental, physical, and social aspect to our lives, we must seek to nourish *all* of who we are. Care must be taken not to neglect any part of our anthropological makeup. To do otherwise denigrates the dignity of our created nature, molded in the image of God himself.

In light of these insights, a number of important questions arise. As far as our physical makeup goes: In what ways have we manifested mistrust and suspicion or even hatred of our bodies? Do we take care of our physical needs (e.g., sufficient sleep, eating well, regular exercise, routine medical checkups)? Have we developed any unhealthy (even addictive) habits? Are we comfortable with what we look like? Are we continually trying by one or another means to look like somebody else? Questions about our mental well-being raise a host of other concerns: Have we been afraid to think for ourselves? (When was the last time you had an original thought?) Do we manifest any overly aggressive behavior (to abuse someone verbally can be just as, if not more, damaging than to do so physically)? Do we allow ourselves to be intimidated by others and made to feel worthless? Do we take time to cultivate the mind (e.g., reading a good book, talking with others about current events, attending lectures or discussions on topics that might interest you)? Care must also be given to our spirits: Do we pray sincerely from the heart? Do we give our spirits the room to yearn for God? Do we spend any time alone — in silence — listening to the stillness of things? Do we listen to the quiet of our own being? Do we seek to befriend the silence that envelops us? Or do we always remain on the surface of life? Finally, there are concerns regarding our social nature: Have we focused too much in the past on our individual needs? Are we prejudiced toward others on religious or ethnic grounds? Do we spend time nurturing sound relationships? Do we make space for others in our lives? Do we recognize the claim of community on our time and efforts? Do we try to identify with and become a part of the social concerns of our community? Are we simply indifferent to the needs of others?

If we are to show hospitality to ourselves, it will be important to try to befriend that part of our human makeup that we find most foreign to us, i.e., the most difficult for us to understand and identify with. Indeed, some of us may feel more at ease spending a quiet evening alone; others may find their element in sports or in enriching the mind, or in an explicitly social gathering. Whatever our strengths, we must learn to befriend the stranger that we are to ourselves and try to nurture in a special way that part which is yet unknown to us and on the periphery of our conscious interest. Ultimately, it is all a question of finding the proper balance that is suited to us as individuals and which acknowledges our indebtedness to community. Arriving at such a balance requires a great deal of practice.

The story of another young girl (this one, by the name of Alice) comes to mind. In her famous adventure through the looking glass, she encounters a cantankerous old knight who is having a rather difficult time staying on top of his horse. After his fifth hurtful tumble, Alice politely remarks, "I'm afraid you've not had much practice in riding." "What makes you say that?" he replies, "I've had *plenty* of practice. . . . The great art of riding is — to keep your balance — properly."[3] With these words he let go of the bridle with both hands stretched out and, as the horse moved, he slipped off and fell on his back, right under the horse's feet!

3. *Befriending the Inner Child.* If such examples from children's literature make any of us feel uneasy, perhaps it is because we ourselves have become estranged from the little child that each of us once was and still carries around inside. "I assure you, unless you change and become like little children, you will not enter the kingdom of God" (Mt 18:3). In what ways have we neglected this child? Have we simply ignored it, leaving it hungry and undernourished or, worse yet, abused and afraid of experiencing life? In what ways is our inner child in need of healing? Do we recognize its importance for our own psychic and spiritual well-being? Do we allow our child to go outside and play with others? Or are we afraid of the world outside or of what others might think of us? Do we listen to that child and try to understand its needs and wants? Do we love our inner child and look forward to spending time in its company? Or have we locked it up somewhere deep inside our unconscious lives, where it screams for attention and care, manifesting itself, at times, in some very childish and destructive ways? Each of us is the parent of the child we once were and hope one day again to become. If we neglect this most basic and fundamental part of ourselves, that underlying dysfunctional relationship will be the basis for many others in the world.

---

[3] Lewis Carroll, *Through the Looking Glass* in *Complete Works* (New York: Vintage Books, 1976), 239-40.

The Stranger in Others

Only by first welcoming and befriending the stranger within will we be able to turn our attention outward and enjoy genuine relationships with those around us. The two main means by which such relationships are forged are those of friendship and community.

1. *Friendship.* I once heard a man say that he could count his real friends on one hand. I remember feeling very sorry for him, for I naively believed at the time that I could be everyone's friend. I concluded that he must have been a very lonely person. As the years passed, I began to see the wisdom of his words: "A faithful friend is a sturdy shelter; he who finds one finds a treasure" (Si 6:14).

A friend, according to Aristotle, is like "a second self," i.e., a single soul existing in two bodies.[4] In the Hebrew tradition, the close, brotherly relationship of David and Jonathan comes to mind: "Jonathan had become as fond of David as if his life depended on him; he loved him as he loved himself" (1 S 18:1-5). Even David and Jonathan, however, were once strangers to one another. There are strangers in the world today who may one day befriend us and become for us a reflection of who we are. The great problem in today's world is that we do not put the time aside to make friends anymore. The fox in Saint Exupéry's *The Little Prince* expresses it well:

> "Men have no more time to understand anything. They buy things all ready made at the shops. But there is no shop anywhere where one can buy friendship, and so men have no friends anymore. If you want a friend, tame me."[5]

---

[4] *Nicomachean Ethics*, 1170b 1-5.

[5] Antoine de Saint Exupéry, *The Little Prince*, trans. Katherine Woods (New York: Harvest Books, 1971), 83-84.

"It is only with the heart that one can see rightly," the fox goes on to say.[6] To many of us, however, the ways of the heart have become a forgotten language. We can no longer see the essential things invisible to the eye; the art of friendship has become an increasingly rare (and therefore highly treasured) craft.

How are we to tame the stranger in our midst? What are the characteristics of a true and lasting friendship? In his book, *The Four Loves*, C.S. Lewis describes friendship as the most spiritual of the natural loves, and therefore the one most easily subject to misunderstanding. Basing himself on the insights of Aristotle, Aquinas, and other classical authors, he describes true friendship as "the least jealous of loves," existing essentially between individuals absorbed in a common interest.[7] A more recent author identifies three marks of genuine friendship: (1) *benevolence*, whereby we actively pursue the well-being of another (as opposed to merely wishing him or her well), (2) *reciprocity*, whereby each person enters freely into the relationship and develops a spirit of mutual concern and affection (in contrast to a purely one-sided relationship that can be frustrating and destructive), and (3) *a mutual indwelling*, whereby each partner in a friendship becomes for the other a reflection of the self (as opposed to the guardedness of strangers and others who pose a threat to us).[8] There are, of course, different degrees of friendships, and the uniqueness of each individual prevents no two relationships between friends from ever being exactly the same. Still, these characteristics must be present in any genuine rapport of friends. These marks are what distinguish our friends from mere acquaintances. The process of taming whereby a stranger becomes first an acquaintance and then a friend will make this fact more and more

---

[6] Ibid., 87.

[7] C.S. Lewis, *The Four Loves* (New York: Harvest Books, 1960), 91-92.

[8] Paul J. Wadell, *Friendship and the Moral Life* (Notre Dame, IN: University of Notre Dame Press, 1989), 130-41.

apparent so that ultimately it becomes only a matter of stating the obvious.

Other questions now come to the surface: Who are our genuine friends? Just how far along the way are we in developing the ties of friendship with others? Do our deepest friendships truly display the important elements of benevolence, reciprocity, and mutual indwelling? Have any of our friendships gone awry? Are any of them abnormally one-sided? Do we comprehend the varying degrees of intimacy and how these enter into the relationships of friends? How do we relate to those with whom we do not wish to be friends? What is the role of friendship in the context of the larger community? The list can go on and on.

2. *Community*. Just as there are varying degrees of friendship so too are there varying degrees of community, as well as varying types. To a great extent, communities are filters through which their members experience and interpret the world around them. They function as a survival mechanism (a "space suit" if you will) that allows us to exist in otherwise inhospitable (even hostile) climates. It goes without saying that the various layers of community surrounding us play a large part in making us the type of persons we have become.

On the level of family, for instance, studies show that no one ever really leaves home. We are all carrying around inside of us the successes and failures of our primary family experience (or lack thereof). It is there, in the home, where we first develop the necessary socialization skills that will be required of us later on in life. Although every family system is in some way flawed (there is only *one* "holy family"), some are more seriously damaged than others ("dysfunctional" so to speak). For this reason, it is important that we ourselves get in touch with and try to change any unhealthy ways of interacting that went on in our primary family during our childhood. It may also be necessary to deal with some of the anger and resentment that we may secretly be venting against our parents (is it right to expect perfection in an imperfect world?). More importantly, we should remember in our dealings with others (and especially those unknown to us) that each person has a unique family history that has a lot to do with the way in which they presently come across. Let us take this background into account when we find ourselves crossing swords with others.

From the family, our communal experiences multiply in various directions. We go to school, join a club or team, go to work and to church; raise families of our own; become members of a political party; get involved with the church, etc. While our primary community experience (that of our family) is always lurking somewhere in the back of our minds, we must also recognize that, for better or worse, our own personalities also come into play. To cite one rather amusing example: Richard Rohr describes the nine Enneagram personalities in terms of animals — "ones" are terriers, ants, and bees; "twos" are donkeys, cats, and puppies; "threes" are chameleons, peacocks, and eagles; "fours" are basset hounds, doves, oysters, and black horses; "fives" are owls, foxes, and hamsters; "sixes" are hares, deer, mice, wolves, and German shepherds; "sevens" are monkeys and butterflies; "eights" are rhinoceroses, rattlesnakes, tigers, and bulls; "nines" are sloths, elephants, dolphins, and whales.[9] Every community is likely to have a variety of personality types from this assorted collection. It should not be surprising, therefore, that a community will resemble at times a jungle (where the law of survival reigns) or, at least, a decidedly cramped rendition of Noah's purportedly spacious Ark (wolves and lambs normally make very poor roommates). When we look at a community, therefore, let us not overlook the individuals who comprise it, and let us also remember that the wolf and lamb will live together in peace only when God's kingdom has become fully manifest (Is 11:6).

---

[9] Richard Rohr and Andreas Ebert, *Discovering the Enneagram* (New York: Crossroad, 1991), 254.

Similar influences come into play in the various levels of Church community, i.e., local, national, and universal. In addition to the family background and different personality types that affect the way we interact on such basic human levels, there are a number of different models of Church that influence our attitudes, i.e., institution, communion, sacrament, herald, and servant.[10] It is very difficult to discern just why a particular person or group will identify the Church with one model over another. The mystery of the Church, to be sure, cannot be exhausted by any one of these models. One may go so far as to say that the great variety of God's creation is reflected even in the many combinations of models that individuals and groups put together in order to express their understanding of Church. In this respect, when we find certain persons expressing an idea of Church other than our own, perhaps it would be best to look upon their opinion as a challenge (rather than a threat) to our attempts at deeper understanding.

Finally, there is the question of to what "world" we belong. The "three worlds" of the free market Western countries (i.e., the first world), the now defunct economic system of the communist bloc (i.e., the second world), and the poor developing countries caught in the middle (i.e., the third world) have been in use for a number of decades and are beginning to lose their usefulness. More recently a "fourth world" has been added to their company, i.e., the poor and marginalized of the first world. What is important for our discussion is the way even these categories (and our reaction to them) have an influence upon the way we relate in community. Anyone who has ever lived in an international community setting (the Roman Generalate of a large religious order, for example) can testify to the tensions and misunderstandings that can exist in an atmosphere where the macrocosm of the world's economic and

---

[10] Popularized by Avery Dulles in *Models of the Church* (Garden City, NY: Doubleday and Co., 1974).

societal structures are projected onto a smaller microcosm of vying personal and national agendas. In such cases, care must be taken to see through the layers of communal experience that make us react the way we do and to try to see beneath everything the dignity of the person before us. The fact that we will fail at times, is no excuse for us not to make the effort. The unhappy alternative is nothing but continual infighting and a growing atmosphere of suspicion and distrust. We deserve better.

As much as we may hate to admit it, we are strangers to many of those who form part of the communities to which we ourselves belong. The more we are able to peer through (if not peel off) the preconceptions of those around us, recognize their inherent human dignity, and welcome them as members on an equal footing, the more closely knit will that community become. If we seek to do this in the presence of others, it is not an unreal expectation to believe that some will recognize our efforts and seek to do likewise. In such a way is the kingdom of God made present in our midst. In such a fashion do we come to experience the presence of God in our lives — and the stranger in God that confronts each one of us.

The Stranger in God

Imagine Moses' surprise when he encountered Yahweh his God in the burning bush (Ex 3:1-6). It must have been a transform-ing experience for him, leaving him with a deepened understand-ing of the utter mystery of the One he served. There, at Horeb, he encountered his God for the first time in his life as a mysterious stranger on the periphery. It was an event not soon to be forgotten.

1. *"Strange gods before Me."* One of the most disturbing stories in the Hebrew Scriptures is the Yahwist's description of the destruction of Sodom (Gn 19:1-29). The abuse intended for the messengers of Yahweh in the opening verses of this account by the

inhabitants of Sodom (vv. 4-5) is a flagrant example of inhospital-
ity meant to be read in direct contrast to the account of Abraham's
hospitality at Mamre in the preceding chapter (Gn 18:1-15). Such
lack of reverence and respect to his messengers is a direct affront to
Yahweh; their lack of hospitality and their failure to recognize God
in the stranger (and, hence, the stranger in God) condemns the
inhabitants of Sodom to an unholy fate.

The story of Sodom challenges us to examine the sometimes
questionable attitudes we have toward God and his messengers. In
what ways do we find ourselves abusing God rather than welcoming
the mystery of his life in our lives? The words of the Torah speak
forcefully to our modern situation:

> "Do not make false gods for yourselves. You shall not erect
> an idol or a sacred pillar for yourselves, nor shall you set up
> a stone figure for worship in your land; for I, the Lord, am
> your God" (Lv 26:1).

Probably the cruelest way in which we abuse God is through the
idols we make of him. Most of us today are too sophisticated to set
up a representation of him of stone or precious metal; cast from a
different mold, our graven images are equally misleading, if not
more. As members of an increasingly bankrupt consumer society,
it is all too easy for us to place the ultimate meaning of our lives in
the acquisition of such transitory things as wealth, honors, fame,
and power. Even those of us with a more explicitly "religious"
approach to life can all too easily *identify* the mystery of God with
the limited doctrinal formulations and norms that have arisen
within the Church for the purpose of guiding us on our journey
homeward. An idolatrous faith has been described as one that
elevates finite realities to the level of ultimate concern.[11] At one

---

[11] Paul Tillich, *Dynamics of Faith* (New York: Harper and Row, 1957), 12.

time or another, all of us have probably succumbed to temptations of this sort.

Two related questions come to mind: What false images of God are operative in our lives? In what ways do we allow the one true God to continue to remain a stranger to us? Is he the good old Uncle George of Gerard W. Hughes' *The God of Surprises*, whom we secretly loathe because he threatens to throw us into a fiery furnace if we fail to do what pleases him? Do we think of him as a policeman, who spends all of his energy pointing out our faults? Or is he a benevolent Santa Claus whom we believed in when we were young but have long since outgrown?[12] Our false images of God are often subtle yet deceptive mental caricatures.

Related to the false images of God that haunt us from our childhood (implanted in us at a vulnerable age by well-meaning but nevertheless misguided parents, teachers, and clergy) is the equally important phenomenon of projection. If we are made in the image of God, why is it that so many of us have it completely the other way around? We spend our time trying to fashion God into a mirror image of ourselves. We do this by throwing our own thoughts, plans, and desires onto a cosmic, providential plane and justify them by invoking the will of God. This usually happens when we fail to take the time in prayer and quiet to properly discern the will of God in our lives. We love taking shortcuts, finding the easy way out. Why waste time with the process of discernment when what we really want is a bottom line that allows us to do what we want? No one, after all, can really show that we have not honestly tried to understand God's will in the matter — no one but God, that is.

Still more questions arise: Do we divinize our own narrowness and self-importance by turning our own wants into a facile identification with those of God? Do we truly encounter God in our lives

---

[12] All of these examples come from Gerard W. Hughes, *The God of Surprises* (London: Darton, Longman and Todd, 1985), 34-36.

as Other or is he nothing more than a reflection of our own over-confident ego? Have we turned God into what nowadays would be called a "wimp" — a big softy who, for lack of courage or fear of being disliked, never challenges anyone? How can we welcome the stranger in God when he whom we worship is nothing more than an inflated image of our own overestimated self-worth? To be hospitable to God we have first to strike down the false images we have of him — regardless of where they come from. We must allow God to be God in our lives.

2. *"The God of Abraham, Isaac and Jacob."* Who is this God we yearn for? How would Abraham, who was asked by God the sacrifice of his only son, respond to such a question? How would Isaac answer, who was tricked into granting his paternal blessing to his second-born? What would Jacob say, who wrestled with the Lord at Peniel? One thing is certain: the God of Abraham, Isaac and Jacob is unpredictably faithful; he cannot be contained; he asks the unexpected of us. He is the God who is what he is — wild and free — a leaping Aslan bounding through the wilds of Narnia, yet ever so careful and gentle with the child riding on his back and holding onto the flowing tufts of his fierce and unwieldy mane. Only when we taste the fierceness and tameness of God — a paradox of such complete and utter mystery to us — can we begin to see the wisdom of the apophatic element of our theological tradition and the way it complements the kataphatic. The name of God is utterable yet unutterable; he manifests himself in the events of history, yet obscures his guiding hand in the same revelatory process. He is utterly beyond us yet mysteriously immanent and simple. He welcomes us before we have even the chance of welcoming him. He is a God of complete and utter graciousness.

3. *The Hospitality of God.* Only by letting God be God in our lives, can we appreciate the many gifts he has bestowed on us. How does he love us? The ways are too innumerable to count. He has blessed us with the wonderful goodness and diversity of his cre-

ation, which comes to us not from necessity, but from his own inner goodness and desire to share. He has placed us at the summit of this creation and fashioned us in his image and likeness. He allows us to be ourselves, to exercise free will; he enables us to enter into bonds of love that reflect the intimacy of his rich inner life. He has sent his Word into our world to befriend us by means of a redeeming message of love. Through the transformation of that life in his death and Resurrection, that Word is even now being born within us and promises to transform us in a life of the Spirit that is beyond our wildest hopes — much like a fairy tale become fact, a dream come true. He has imparted his Spirit to us in order to inspire us to follow the stillness of his voice in our adventure through life. He has provided us with food and drink for our journey and promises to guide us as we find our long way back home. God's hospitality to us bespeaks boundless care and generosity! It is another word for grace.

Conclusion

Welcoming the stranger in our lives — be it within ourselves, in others, or in God — is a concrete way by which we affirm the deep desire in each of us to share with others the wonderful grace given to us by God. If the good truly is self diffusive (as the philosophers tell us), then the degree of hospitality that we show to others will be proportionate to the degree of intimacy that we have come to share with God. The process of our divinization, in other words, is intimately related to the atmosphere of human warmth and wel-come that we create for those around us and especially for the stranger in our midst. If, in God's eyes, we are not just strangely familiar, but always deeply reverenced and welcome to become a part of his own inner circle of intimate friends, then as "the friends of God" we are always encouraged to follow suit whenever such an opportunity arises. The mission of God's People, the Church, is to make this circle of friends an ever wider reality in the present and to look forward to its fullest expansion in the reign of the kingdom that is to come.

Hospitality is such a universal trait of human culture because it is so utterly familiar to God himself, who fashioned us in his image. Despite the ravages of war and injustice in our imperfect world, we possess in our collective memory a vague recollection of what paradise must be like: enemies lay down their weapons; stranger befriends stranger; friend breaks bread with friend. *Hospes*, the Latin root of the word (meaning, "stranger or friend, foreigner, host, or guest") reveals the eschatological orientation of this deepest of human longings. Human hospitality is but a shallow reflection of that which we find in God. But it *is* a reflection — and it can be brightened and even transformed. God has a way of bringing the best out of our humanity and turning it into the most precious of pearls.

During our lifetimes, unfamiliar faces are always emerging from the crowd and entering into the periphery of our awareness. How we welcome them and the initiative we take to do so reveals much about our relationship with God and our commitment to work for the establishment of his kingdom. These figures may arrive at any time and in the most unexpected of places: within the self, in those around us, in God himself. Wherever and whenever we encounter them, they are to be received as Christ would receive them. Such is the common call of all who look to him and invoke his name.

Book ix

Befriended By Silence

$\quad$ ounds would make little sense to us if they were not heard
$\quad$ against a stable, yet unassuming, backdrop of silence. It is
$\quad$ silence which brings the words we speak, the songs we sing,
the games we play, into sharp, recognizable relief. Without it, life
would be a continuous barrage of incessant clamor. Incapable of
distinguishing even the slightest audible note, we would be left
helpless, unable to draw connections and, hence, utterly incapable
of communicating with other people, let alone with ourselves, or
with God. Silence is the ground of our experience, the *sine qua non*
for all dignified human relations. It beckons us out of awareness and
into rest, offering us, through varying degrees of encounter, a
deeper knowledge of who we are and of those whose lives we touch.

1. Awareness

Because we tend to concentrate on making sense out of the
sounds we hear, most of us are usually not aware of the extent to
which silence penetrates our lives. It is much easier to listen to the
beat of a drum or to the tick of a clock than to the silence which
makes them possible. When those moments do arrive that our

attention focuses on what lies behind all that reaches our ears, many of us are caught unawares and left uncertain as to how to respond.

"The Spirit blows wherever it wills. . . ." Be it late at night in the heavy pounding of our hearts, or when we pause momentarily to observe the pregnant stillness in our rooms; be it between the casual sips of our morning coffee, in the fervent throes of mental prayer, or beneath the ominous gaze of a star-studded sky — wherever it blows, to become aware of the silence in our lives and of how it permeates everything we do is to resonate in being with all existing things and to reverence the presence of God's Spirit within us, who works quietly, undisturbed, deep within the recesses of our hearts.

It is there, in the silence, where we hear our spirits yearning for what lies beyond. It is there, in the silence, where we discover the insignificance of ourselves before the divine. It is there, in the silence, where we find ourselves making the first faint overtures of prayer. It is there, in the silence, where we first discover why "the first shall be last" and why "the last shall be first." It is there, in the silence, where, for the slightest part of a moment, we get in touch with our deeper selves and begin (perhaps for the first time in our lives) to place the needs of others before our own.

2. Listening

It is not enough merely to advert to the silence or simply to recognize its existence as the backdrop of all human intercourse. As the veritable starting point of prayer, it beckons us to enter into relationship with it: to listen to it and to be listened to by it. Such a relationship means a heightened awareness of the emptiness within ourselves, an emptiness which can be filled only by itself and which spills over into the well of divinity that sustains it and gives it being. We must dialogue with the silence — speak to it.

For lack of better tools, we may at first need recourse to words. These should be few and well chosen, meant not to get in the way, but to articulate the inner movement of our hearts. By this entering into dialogue with the silence, we befriend it by not being scared by it; by allowing ourselves to rest in it. We slowly begin to realize that silence accompanies us throughout our lives and that, try as we may, we cannot escape its persistent, omnipresent gaze. We enter into dialogue with the silence, we befriend it, by not running away from it, by listening to it. In doing so, we slowly begin to recognize that silence is not something exterior to the self to be afraid of, but actually a part of ourselves, the very part which roots the self in the divine and which holds out to us the hope of our final transformation.

In listening to the silence and by adverting to it wherever we go, we experience life in a different way. We move through time in constant dialogue with the silence which supports the self and all that lies beyond it. This helps us to befriend the world, to listen to it, to become a part of it, and it to become a part of us. Through our listening, we find a basis for solidarity with others and with the world at large. We discover that silence everywhere abounds — at all places, in all circumstances, in all hearts. Through such awareness, we see ourselves in close proximity to all things: living and non-living alike. We find ourselves moving towards the ground which sustains all of reality: a ground outside the self and the world, yet in the self and in the world. In listening to the silence, we receive a deeper awareness of the ground of our being and of all the world. In befriending the silence, we enter into intimacy with the ground of all things and slowly discover that, by our very own existing, that same ground has, all the while, been befriending the likes of us.

3. Yearning

Silence speaks to us through yearning. Those who listen to the silence around them, who befriend the silence which otherwise gnaws at them in loneliness, feel in the core of the self the solitary ache of all existing things. Always present, but seldom attended to, this ache is the common means of intercourse between ourselves and the divine. Created by God, we feel our limitations in the face of infinite possibility. The Spirit of God stirs within us and resonates in the silence of our souls. This silence fills us and reveals to us our own insecurity, our own incompleteness, our own frailty and fragile nature. It is through yearning that we, in befriending the silence, first experience the movement of God's Spirit in our lives. The Spirit, who groans within us and yearns for our complete and final union with God, moves beneath the silence of our hearts. From there, it carries our natural aching and inner yearnings to a point beyond ourselves, where our spirits touch God's Spirit and where both commune in silence in the single embrace of God's primal creative groan: "All of creation groans . . ." "The Spirit groans within. . ." "Oh Lord, my soul will not rest . . . ."

It is in our yearning that we learn of our divine destiny. Our heartfelt aching for what will complete us points out the way for our own self-transcendence. Our yearning leads us along the way of the cross to a point beyond the grave, when death no longer threatens and where fear no longer thrives. Those who dare to yearn follow the faint, glimmering light of a distant guiding star. To ache with that light, to howl at its moonlight reflection in the self, to be one with all of humanity, all of nature, all of the world — to be alive! "It is no longer I who live. . . ."

Death approaches; life subsides — yet withstands. Rising out of the ashes comes an ever-deepening silence which, born from the human heart, cannot be silenced, and which renders us still before our deepest fears, our innermost aches and yearnings, before our

God. It is God who created us in the silence of his own heart, who yearned for our existence from all eternity and who regards us in the gaze of death with the heartbreak of a grieving parent. Our yearnings tell us of God's ache for us. It is he who fashioned us in the silence, creating us in his image — "out of the clay of the ground."

4. Probing

We now probe deeply into yet unchartered corners of our souls. We search through and become aware of needs and desires that we never knew we had. We begin to appreciate more and more the people who have helped us in our journey through life. Such probing gives us a deeper knowledge of ourselves and of those who have touched our lives. We become attuned more and more to the bond that we share with all people. Differences that separate us diminish in the light of our common dignity as human beings sustained from moment to moment by a benevolent God in the silence of his own becoming.

We probe not only ourselves, but also those around us. Their needs become our needs; their desires, our own desires. We seek to be with them in spirit, no matter what distances may separate us. We nurture an openness towards everyone we meet. Every stranger becomes an unmet friend; every friend, a window to eternity. We probe the depths of another's heart and find there the silence of our own and the quiet, unobtrusive presence of the benevolent God himself. In probing our own hearts and those of whom we love, we find ourselves moving ever more deeply into the heart of the very same God who creates, sustains, and nourishes us. It is he who, from all eternity, has probed our every need and desire. It is he who, to understand us more fully, became one of us in the person of Jesus of Nazareth.

To know ourselves better, to know and understand others more deeply, is to discover the reality of Christ in our lives and to enter more deeply into the intimate relationship that we share with his Father. The active self-probing which spawns from our listening to and yearning with the silence in our hearts has become a window through which we peer into the divinity of God and the promise of our own future divinization in Christ. It is a means through which we transcend ourselves by ultimately forgetting ourselves in the search for that which lies beyond the self and beyond the silence within the self — the love of God made manifest in the life and death of Jesus Christ. "A man has no greater love. . . ."

5. Asking

This deeper awareness of ourselves brings us to a deeper awareness of God's presence in our lives as the ground of our being. We are eventually moved to direct our needs towards him, confident that they will be heard: "Where two or three of you are gathered in my name . . ." "Anything that you ask the Father in my name. . . ."

The prayer of petition flows from the yearning and probing of our befriended silence: Christ is the bond that spans the abyss between the self and the other. It is his Spirit who moves the heart to ask God for forgiveness, for our daily bread, for his kingdom to come. It is his Spirit who moves us to bring the needs of others to God in prayer. These requests may or may not involve explicit words, thoughts, or sentiments. Consciously, we may not even know what to pray for or whom to pray for. But the Spirit of Christ within us speaks the unutterable when it moves our spirits to the praise, glory, and honor of God and asks on our behalf for the fulfillment of our deepest yearnings and desires.

Asking comes easily for those who have befriended the

silence. They have learned to listen and to yearn in the quiet of their hearts. In the process, they have come to befriend and be befriended by the Lord of Silence himself: "I no longer call you slaves. . . ."

6. Resting

We have reached a point where we feel at ease with the silence in our hearts. It has befriended us and has brought us rest. We feel at peace with ourselves, with others, and with God. We now face the silence without feeling threatened by it. We know that we are known and that someone else knows all there is to know about us. There is no need to hide. The silence has penetrated all of our masks and self-deceptions. It is there, with us, as we really are. It has neither abandoned us nor forsaken us. Rather, it refreshes us in its warm and tender embrace.

Resting in the silence revives us. It recreates our inner powers and enables us to continue with renewed vigor and strength. In being recreated, we are able to leave the silence and gaze upon those around us in a different light. Aware of the weariness and loneliness that so many others experience in their lives, we try to direct them to the hidden spring of God's inner silence.

To drink from the silence; to bathe in the silence; to be cleansed, purged in the silence; to be born in the silence. "Unless a man be born again. . . ." Even the words of Jesus take on new meaning. Wrought from his own encounter with the depths of silence, they come alive only when heard with the sensitivity of his own heart. To drink from the silence, to rest in the silence, "to be born again," is to enter once again that womb of silence whence we have come and will all eventually return. "The kingdom of God is within you. . . ." Full rest — eternal rest — is God's promise to all who, like his only begotten Son, have befriended the silence within them and seek to live in the quiet of its peace. Such is our human journey: out of awareness, into rest — to the peace of God's kingdom.

The Purest Gold

There once was a young man from the distant but not so far away town of Everywhere, who was intent on spending his entire life in search of the end of a rainbow and its fabled pot of gold. Since rainbows with their colorful beginnings, middles, and ends (just which end is the beginning and which is the end is rather difficult to say) can occur, depending on the position of the sun, the beckoning of the sky, and the magic in the air, in nearly every land, and with the possibility of its beginning (or ending, as the case may be) in nearly any place, the young man set out on a journey to the town of Nowhere-In-Particular, which borders the famed country of Anywhere-At-All. The young man was rather boyish and of the whimsical sort. And he was a great talker. Throughout his journey, he did nothing but talk about the great fortune he was going to find, about what he was going to be when he found it, about what he was going to do with it when he had it in his hands, about the women, the wine, the travel, the food, and countless other things! Indeed, he talked so fast and about so many things that even the best of listeners had a difficult time understanding him. As a matter of fact, sometimes the young man did not even know what he himself was saying! This explains the rather puzzled and uncertain look that fell over his face when he talked.

And since he talked nearly all the time (and mostly to himself, one might add), it is little wonder that he soon came to be known by the name "Puzzles."

At the beginning of one particular day, Puzzles was just about to resume his whimsical way towards Nowhere-In-Particular and the land of Anywhere-At-All when a peculiar thing happened! The magic in the air began to stir the morning sky. The sky beckoned the sun, and the sun cast a beautiful rainbow over the still, quiet earth. Now Puzzles, who even at this early hour was already too busy talking to himself to notice the beauty of the moment, just happened to be standing on the very spot of land where the end of the rainbow was touching ground. For a few precious moments, the rainbow hovered over this small speck of earth and covered it with its soft, luminous rays. The astonished Puzzles was bathed in beams of multicolored light and seemed almost to drop out of sight! As, indeed, he did! Just as all things of enchantment must sooner or later return to the distant but not so far away land from whence they come, this beautiful rainbow, whose end had found the whimsical Puzzles, soon began to fade away and return to the home that it shared with the sun, the sky, and the magic in the air. What happened next occurred so quickly and so mysteriously that even the keenest observer would scarce believe his eyes. At the final moment of its earthly appearance, when the beautiful rainbow was barely visible in the crisp morning air beneath the sun, it bequeathed its last touch of magic to the world by penetrating the now thoroughly puzzled Puzzles and turning him into a huge slab of granite rock!

At first, Puzzles did not know what happened to him. He tried to move his arms, but he did not have any arms to move! He then tried to walk, but he did not have any legs to do the walking! He then tried to turn his head, but he did not have a head, or even a neck to do the turning! Worst of all, when he tried to open his lips and move his tongue to say something, he discovered that, not having anything that resembled a lip or a tongue, he could not even talk! As a rock, about the only thing that Puzzles could do was think. He had no arms or legs to move, no head to turn, no eyes to see with, no nose to smell with or ears to hear with, and no fingers to touch with! Just about all he could do was think! And the only reason why he could think was because, while his body was now that of a rock, the magic of the rainbow had somehow allowed his soul to remain that of a man. As one might well imagine, Puzzles was by this time not only puzzled but also heartbroken, and lonely, and downright sad. He had wanted to be many things in life, but never in all his wildest dreams had he ever so much as entertained the idea of being a rock! Life as a rock, he imagined, could not be anything but exceedingly dull. And so Puzzles prepared himself for an eternity of endless boredom. For lack of anything better (or, for that matter, "anything at all") to do, he spent his days and a good part of his nights (rocks require very little sleep) in thought.

Much to the surprise and puzzlement of Puzzles, life as a rock was not really that bad after all! Of course, during his first few years he had a difficult time adjusting to a life whose only outlet was that of thought, but he gradually adapted himself to the circumstances at hand and, believe it or not, actually began to like being a rock! He looked forward to his days and would often find himself thinking into the wee hours of the morning. He thought about just about everything there was to think about. And, when he had finished his thinking for the night, he would take a short nap, awaken, and find still more things upon which he could ponder and reflect. He thought about himself and about his dreams, of how he had lived his life as a man, about what he would do over again if he had the chance. He thought about all the people that he had ever met, and of the countless others he had not so much as even seen! He thought about his family and his friends, about his home and his country, about the earth and the sky, the oceans and the seas, the mountains, the deserts and the plains! He thought about everything under the sun, and everything over the sun as well! He pondered everything in the universe, including the moon, the stars, the galaxies, and the endless space! Sometimes he would lose himself in such a deep state of thought that he did not even feel like a rock! Instead, in a strange and mysterious sort of way, he felt as if he were everywhere and nowhere at the same time — and everyone who was breathing at that very moment! Those were the times he liked best. They did not come often (actually, they were very few and far between), but they were well worth the wait. For Puzzles, those special moments were the part about being a rock he liked best.

Years passed — ninety-nine to be exact. By this time, Puzzles had grown quite used to living his life in thought. He liked being a rock and, as a matter of fact, he could barely remember what it was like not being a rock! His many years of contemplation and thought had brought him wisdom. And not only that! Even though his rocky slab was very much weathered and more than a little worn, he was just about as happy as a great slab of granite rock could ever possibly be!

It just so happened that at the beginning of another particular day — the very day which marked the ninety-ninth year of Puzzles' entry into rockdom — another peculiar thing happened! Once again the magic in the air began to stir the morning sky. Once more the sky beckoned the sun. And the sun once again cast a beautiful rainbow over the still, quiet earth with its end touching ground on the very spot where Puzzles had stood so many years before and where he now lay as a rock deep in the depths of the deepest thought. Once again the rainbow covered Puzzles with its multicolored rays of light. And once again, when it was barely visible in the crisp morning air beneath the sun and was ready to return to the distant but not so far away land from whence it came, it bequeathed its last touch of magic to the world by touching the pondering

Puzzles, shaking his worn and weathered rock granite slab, and turning him back into a man!

Ninety-nine years, while bringing Puzzles both wisdom and happiness, had taken its toll in age. Puzzles was now an old man with wrinkled skin, a stooping back and a long flowing beard of white. He sat with his eyes closed as still and as silent as a rock itself. Then, slowly, he began to realize what had happened. First he could feel the air enter and fill him within, and he knew he could breathe! Then, he could feel strength come back to reappearing limbs, and he knew that he could move! He moved his tongue and his lips, and he knew that he could talk! Finally, he opened his eyes and knew that he could see! And lo and behold! Right between his legs, before his very eyes, sitting on the very spot where he had spent countless hours in the depths of the deepest thought, was a pot of pure nugget gold! Puzzles had found the end of a rainbow! He had finally found its pot of gold!

Perhaps even more peculiar is what Puzzles did with the pot of gold once he found it. Rather than spending it, or saving it by savagely guarding it with his life, or even burying it so that no one else could find it, he simply and quite unreservedly gave it away — one nugget at a time — to every boyish young man who happened down the road. With the gift of a nugget, Puzzles would open his lips, let out a deep but silent sigh, and speak in a low, quiet whisper the following words: "A purer gold than this is at the rainbow's end. Go find it, my son. Go and find it." Now no young man, wherever he came from, be it near or far, from Everywhere or from Nowhere-In-Particular, or perhaps even from Anywhere-At-All, could quite understand the meaning of what Puzzles had told him. What gold could possibly be purer than the very nugget in his hand? No gold is purer than pure gold itself! No one understood the words of the old man; the meaning of the phrase eluded every hearer. Yet, regardless of whether or not anyone understood him, every young man, attracted by the gleam and glitter of the pure nugget gold, set out — each in his own whimsical and rather boyish sort of way — to find the end of a rainbow and the gold that was purer than gold itself. The old man, to be sure, was very strange indeed! He spoke so rarely, so quietly, and so mysteriously! And, when he did speak, it was only about the rainbow's end and the purer gold than gold! Every day and nearly every night he simply sat on that single spot of land, lost in the deepest depths of thought, waiting for the next young traveler to pass him on the road. Since no one understood him, it is little wonder that he soon came to be known by the name of "The Puzzler."

Years passed. Little by little the Puzzler had given away every nugget from his fortune of gold. All during this time no one had ever dared try to rob him, for he looked so strange and mysterious and he spoke so seldom that everyone thought he was possessed by a strange sort of magic. And indeed he was. He now spent his days sitting on his small spot of land, leaving it only to take a small bit of bread or broth, which some kind traveler had given him, or to go inside an old wooden shed just beyond the place where he sat to lie down on a small straw bed. Sometimes he would spend the entire day and even the entire night simply sitting outside on his small spot of land. He would do nothing but close his eyes, listen to the silence within himself, and think beyond the deepest thought.

The Puzzler continued living his life of solitude to a ripe old age. He actually became a legend in his own time. People came from far and near, from Everywhere and from Nowhere-In-Particular (and some even from Anywhere-At-All), to see him and, they hoped, to hear him speak. When the moment finally came that the old man's breathing grew faint, and when his eternal ponderings could no longer continue within his earthly frame, he quietly sighed a silent sigh and opened his eyes to the morning sun. He could feel the magic of the air stir the sky, and he heard the sky beckon the sun. He then opened his lips, slowly moved his tongue

— and spoke not a word. He simply smiled, closed his eyes, breathed his final breath, and died. As with the rainbow and as with all things of enchantment, the old Puzzler returned to the distant but not so far away land from whence he came.

He was buried on the small spot of land which had been his home (and much more) for so very many years. He died a very old man, indeed. No one knew just where he came from. Legend says he appeared one day out of Nowhere-In-Particular and lived where he died for the rest of his earthly days. Legend also says that he died as old and as wise as eternity itself — and that he died content. Fittingly enough, an unknown traveler marked his grave on the small spot of land with a huge slab of granite rock. Cut into the stone was the following epitaph:

> Here lies, "The Puzzler,"
> Who at the rainbow's end
> Found a purer gold than gold.

To this very day, young men read these words when they pass the Puzzler's grave. Many of them, filled with dreams of fortune and success, have set out in search of the rainbow and its fabled pot of gold. None of them have been seen or heard of again. Even to this day the Puzzler's words remain shrouded in mystery.

On certain days, when the magic in the air stirs the morning sky and the sky beckons the sun from afar, a rainbow will appear over the still, quiet earth with its end touching ground on the old Puzzler's grave. It lingers playfully for a few moments, as if in silent veneration of its old pondering friend. Then, before departing to its home with the sun, the sky, and the magic in the air, it covers the old man's grave with its multicolored rays of light, leaving the world with its last touch of magic.